sew small

19 little bags

stash your coins, keys,
earbuds, jewelry & more

jennifer heynen

stash BOOKS®

an imprint of C&T Publishing

Text copyright © 2017 by Jennifer Heynen

Photography and artwork copyright © 2017 by C&T Publishing, Inc.

Publisher: Amy Marson

Creative Director: Gailen Runge

Editors: Liz Aneloski and Donna di Natale

Technical Editors: Del Walker and Linda Johnson

Cover/Book Designer: April Mostek

Production Coordinator: Zinnia Heinzmann

Production Editor: Jennifer Warren

Illustrator: Kirstie L. Pettersen

Photo Assistants: Carly Jean Marin and Mai Yong Vang

Style photography by Lucy Glover and instructional photography by
Diane Pedersen of C&T Publishing, Inc., unless otherwise noted

Published by Stash Books, an imprint of C&T Publishing, Inc., P.O. Box 1456,
Lafayette, CA 94549

Library of Congress Cataloging-in-Publication Data

Names: Heynen, Jennifer, author.

Title: Sew small : 19 little bags : stash your coins, keys, earbuds, jewelry &
more / Jennifer Heynen.

Other titles: 19 little bags

Description: Lafayette, CA : C&T Publishing, Inc., 2017.

Identifiers: LCCN 2016041231 | ISBN 9781617454332 (soft cover)

Subjects: LCSH: Bags. | Sewing.

Classification: LCC TT667 .H49 2017 | DDC 646.4/8--dc23

LC record available at https://lccn.loc.gov/2016041231

Printed in China

10 9 8 7 6 5 4 3 2 1

dedication

This book is dedicated to my family:

Nik, Fletcher, and Birkley.

acknowledgments

I would like to thank my entire

C&T family. You make writing a book

fun. Special thanks to the members

I work with the most: Gailen, Roxane,

Liz, Lynn, and Deirdre.

contents

Introduction   6

Fabrics   8

Ribbons, Threads, and Trims   10

Buttons, Beads, and More   12

Attaching Embellishments   14

About the Author   111

projects

PROJECTS

introduction

A little bag is one of my favorite things to sew. Making a cute little zippered pouch is a great way to spend an afternoon, and when you're finished, you've got something useful that will keep your things where they need to be. This book is full of bags to hold brushes, earbuds, chargers, journal supplies, money, and more.

a place for everything

● ●

I don't know about you, but I am constantly making or buying little bags and pouches for everything I carry. There's just something about having the perfectly sized and shaped bag to hold exactly what you need. Clip the Ladybug Bag to a backpack and always know where your cord is when you need it. Carry your mending supplies in the Drawstring House Bag.

pretty practical

● ●

If you're going to use a small bag to carry your things and use them every day, then it should definitely be cute. There's no reason a practical bag can't be pretty as well. You'll smile every time you pack your flip-flops in your Flip-Flop Travel Bag.

great gifts

Little bags also make great gifts. How cute would the Birdcage Bag be as a gift filled with a couple of bottles of nail polish—or the Whale Coin Purse, filled with birthday money for a special little someone?

make it your own

All of these bags have embellishments or appliqués, but feel free to experiment with different fabrics and embellishments. Make the Wallet Clutch in denim, faux leather, or a fabric that matches your favorite dress. Slip a picture in with the glitter when making the Clear Zipper Pouch.

have fun

As always, I hope you smile a little when you're making these bags. Please show me your creations, tagged with #littlebags on Instagram. I look forward to seeing what you sew!

fabrics

(A) COTTON

I find myself in awe of how many designs and colors are available in cotton fabrics for quilting. Fabrics that are 100% cotton or cotton blends wash well and are the perfect weight for the projects in this book.

(B) WOOL

Wool is yet another fun fabric to keep on hand for adding texture. Some companies dye beautiful plain and patterned wools in a huge variety of colors. I use just about any kind of wool I can get my hands on if I like the color.

(C) TULLE

I use tulle for adding ruffles and textured layers in flowers. Tulle is inexpensive, so it's easy to keep a variety of colors on hand. Most tulle you find in stores is standard lightweight tulle. Milliners usually carry heavier weight tulle as well.

(D) VELVETEEN

Velveteen is a soft fabric. With a tighter weave than velvet, it doesn't fray as easily. It's usually available in fabric stores in just a few colors. From time to time, I dye velveteen yardage to keep on hand for embellishing. Be sure to stock up on white or ivory for custom dyeing.

(E) VELVET

Velvet has texture and rich color. It's a very soft fabric that can be a bit tricky to sew because it is silky and can fray at the edges. To keep things less complicated, I use velvet in flowers and other small embellishments.

(F) FELT

Be sure to keep lots of different colors of felt on hand. I prefer using 100% wool or a wool-blend felt. These are softer and cut much more nicely than polyester craft felt. I encourage you to try it if you never have; you'll be amazed how pleasant it is to sew.

ribbons, threads, and trims

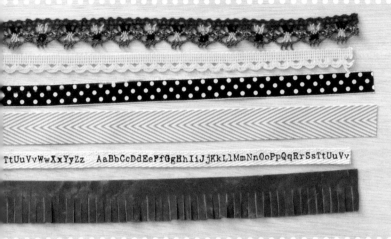

TRIMS

There are so many trims on the market that I can't even begin to tell you about all the different kinds. Crocheted trims and fringes are a few of my favorites. Grosgrain and silk ribbons come printed and woven in a variety of colors, and because they are flat, they are easy to sew onto your project. Head to the notions area of your favorite quilt shop to see what you can find.

RICKRACK

Rickrack is another one of my favorites to keep on hand. I collect many different sizes and colors. Rickrack starts small, at ¼″ wide, and goes all the way to 1½″ wide. Sometimes I shop on Etsy (etsy.com) for vintage rickrack that comes in colors and textures that are no longer available.

VELVET RIBBON

Velvet ribbon is one of those trims that automatically adds texture and depth to a project. The colors are very rich.

POM-POM TRIM

Pom-pom trim adds instant fun to any project. I love collecting all sizes and colors. I have even been known to layer pom-pom trims—I like them that much. Like rickrack, they come in a huge range of sizes and colors.

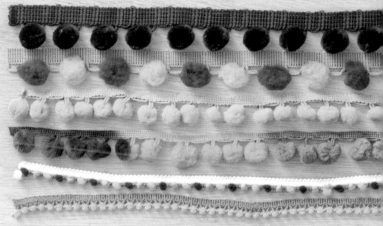

SIX-STRAND FLOSS

Six-strand embroidery floss comes in a huge variety of colors. You can use one to six strands at a time. Most of the time, I use all six strands when embellishing.

THREE-STRAND FLOSS

I admit that I am a lazy stitcher. Some flosses now come in three strands, so they don't need to be separated. I keep a handful of my favorite colors on hand so they are ready for hand stitching. Three-strand floss is nice to use when you want your stitches to show but don't want heavy six-strand stitches.

buttons, beads, and more

BUTTONS AND BEADS

Buttons and beads are so much fun to collect that most likely I don't need to give you a reason to get some. I pick them up anytime I find some that are interesting. Buttons and beads come in glass, metal, wood, plastic, Bakelite, and more. I love to use a mix of them all.

FELT BALLS

When I think of felt balls, I think of three-dimensional polka dots. Felt balls come in a variety of colors and sizes. Sometimes you can find them with stripes, polka dots, or embellishments. They are not beads and therefore do not have holes in them. This is great because they can be sewn on in any way you like. Felt balls can also be embroidered for more fun.

YARN POM-POMS AND TASSELS

Pom-poms and tassels go hand in hand with felt balls as embellishments. Tassels add great texture to your bags. They are readily available in many colors and materials.

attaching embellishments

machine topstitching

You can add a lot of decoration and interest to your project quickly by using your sewing machine. Topstitching can be done just by using the straight stitch and outlining the appliqué in coordinating or black thread. The stitching lines may be stitched over a time or two, depending on how noticeable you want the stitching to be. If you're lucky enough to have a machine with decorative stitches, these may be used for embellishing as well.

To attach ribbon, sew down each side. It's best to sew from the top to the bottom on each side instead of turning around and sewing in the opposite direction. Sometimes ribbons have stretch, and stitching in the same direction on both sides will prevent the ribbon from becoming distorted. Stitching close to the edge helps the ribbon to lie flat.

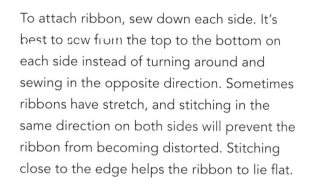

Topstitching rickrack is tricky because it curves, and you can't just sew along the curves unless it's jumbo rickrack (or you have a lot of time and patience). One option is to sew straight down the middle and leave each side free to curl. I find what I like best is to sew a rickrack in two or three places, depending on the width. This holds the trim in place and adds a bit more detail.

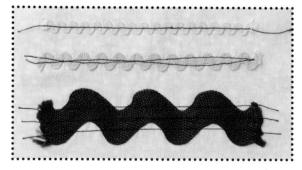

adding edge trim with machine stitching

When adding edge trims, your first instinct might be to place the trim right along the edge of the fabric. Instead, you should measure ¼˝ in from the edge; this is where the construction stitching will be. To position your trim, find the edge or center of the trim—or wherever you want the construction stitching to be—and place it just over the ¼˝ line but within the seam allowance. The trim that is outside the seam allowance will be visible.

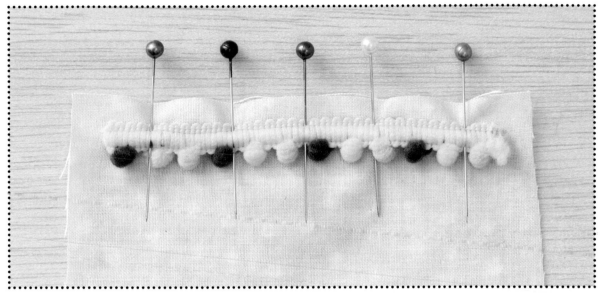

Pin the trim.

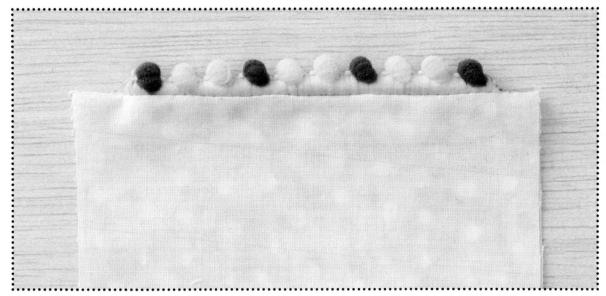

Finished seam with edge trim

hand stitching

Hand stitching is sometimes the easiest way to attach a stack of decorative fabrics to a project. I like to keep a variety of needles on hand for that purpose. Small super-sharp needles are great for stitching openings closed, whereas a larger soft-sculpture doll needle is great for sewing wider items.

When sewing on a felt ball, whether a half or a whole one, I choose a sewing thread that matches the ball. Just sew through the base of the project, and then push the needle through the ball approximately ¼″ from ball's edge and out the opposite side to secure. Send the needle back into the base, and repeat this stitch a few times to secure the ball. If the felt ball is cut in half, sew through the project and send the needle through the edge of the base and back out and through the project again. Sew all the way around the base to secure.

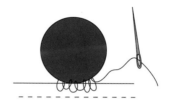

embroidery

Lots of books are available on embroidery, as well as online tutorials. I won't go into a lot of detail about stitches, but here are some of the basic stitches I use.

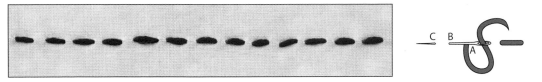

Running stitch

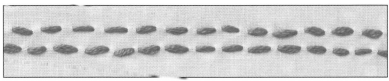

Zipper stitch (2 rows of running stitches)

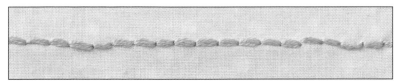

Backstitch

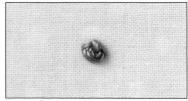
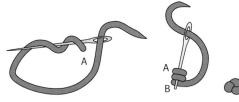

French knot

card holder

FINISHED SIZE: 2½″ × 4″

materials

- 8–10 scraps of quilting cotton, at least 1½″ × 3½″ each, for outer shell and tab

- ⅛ yard *or* 1 fat quarter of quilting cotton for lining

- ⅛ yard of batting to add padding to bag

- 1″ × 3″ sew-on leather snap fastener (3DANsupplies on Etsy)

- 4″ of ball-chain key chain

- All-purpose sewing thread to match lining

cutting

OUTER SHELL

- 16 pieces 1½″ × 1½″

TAB

- 1 piece 2″ × 2″

LINING

- 2 pieces 2½″ × 4½″

BATTING

- 2 pieces 2½″ × 4½″

instructions

Seam allowances are ¼″.

1. Sew 4 rows of 4 different 1½″ × 1½″ squares each. Press the seams open. *Fig. A*

2. Sew 2 rows together to create a 2½″ × 4½″ rectangle. Press the seams open. Repeat. *Fig. B*

3. Sew a 2½″ × 4½″ piece of batting to the wrong side of each pieced rectangle, either by stitching ⅛″ around the edge or in the ditch between the squares.

4. Sew a lining piece to the top of each rectangle from Step 2, right sides together. Press the seams open and set aside. *Fig. C*

5. Fold the 2″ × 2″ tab piece in half and press. Open the piece up and fold the raw edges of 2 sides in to meet the fold. Press and fold in half again. *Fig. D*

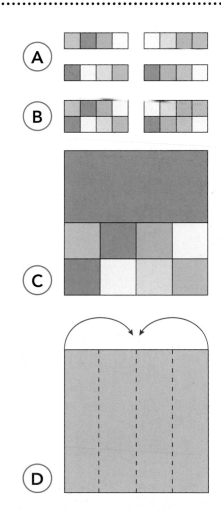

6. Edgestitch down each side of the tab. Fold in half. Pin the tab just above the centerline on the side, as shown. *Fig. E*

7. Align the lining and the front outer shell with right sides together, matching the middle seam. Sew around the edge, leaving an opening in the lining for turning. Clip the corners and turn right side out through the opening. *Fig. F*

8. Hand stitch the opening closed. Push the lining into the holder.

9. Hand stitch the leather strap and magnet onto the holder. The placement will be determined by the length of the strap and whether you're holding business or loyalty cards. *Fig. G*

TIP : Place your cards into the holder to determine the best placement for the sew-on leather fastener.

10. Slide the chain through the loop; fasten.

E
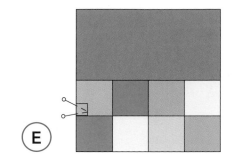

F
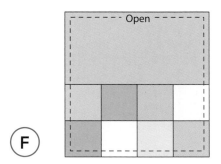

G
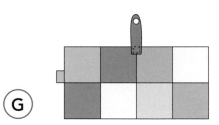

key-ring coin purse

FINISHED SIZE: 2″ × 3″

materials

- ⅛ yard *or* 1 fat quarter of quilting cotton or linen for outer shell
- ⅛ yard *or* 1 fat quarter of quilting cotton for lining
- 6″ × 6″ faux leather for corners
- 5″ × 10″ medium-weight fusible interfacing
- 6″ zipper
- 1½″ key ring
- 6-strand floss in 5 colors
- Transfer pen or water-soluble paper
- Embroidery hoop

cutting

OUTER SHELL

- 2 pieces 4″ × 4½″

LINING

- 2 pieces 4″ × 4½″

FAUX LEATHER

- 4 pieces using the Key-Ring Coin Purse corner pattern (pullout page P1)
- 1 piece 2″ × ½″

MEDIUM-WEIGHT FUSIBLE INTERFACING

- 2 pieces 4″ × 4½″

instructions

Seam allowances are ¼″.

1. Before cutting the fabric, transfer the Key-Ring Coin Purse flower pattern (pullout page P1) onto the *right* side of 1 outer shell piece. Using 6 strands of floss and referring to the photo, embroider the flower on the outer shell piece.

2. Iron the interfacing to the reverse side of the outer shell fabric. Stitch the faux leather corner pieces to the front and back outer shell pieces. *Fig. A*

3. Run the faux leather strip through the key ring and pin to hold. Pin the strap to the center of the front outer shell piece. Make sure to pin the ring facing inward. *Fig. B*

4. Lay an outer shell piece right side up on your work surface. Place the zipper, teeth down, across the top of the fabric with the zipper centered. Pin in place. *Fig. C*

5. Place a piece of lining fabric, right side down, on top of the pinned zipper. Make sure to match the top and side edges of the outer shell fabric and the lining. Pin in place. *Fig. D*

6. Sew through all layers using the zipper foot on your machine.

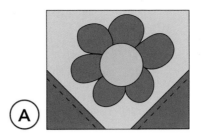

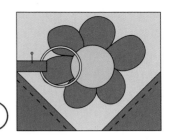

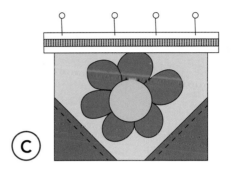

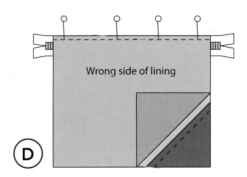

7. Fold each fabric back from the zipper so that the outer shell and lining are wrong sides together. Place the remaining side of the zipper facedown onto the right side of the remaining outer shell piece. Pin in place. Place the lining on top of the zipper. Pin in place and sew down the second side of the zipper.

8. Arrange and pin the right sides of the outer shell fabric together and the lining together. Starting at the bottom of the lining, sew around the outside of the coin purse, leaving approximately a 2″ gap for turning, as shown. *Fig. E*

9. Clip the corners and turn right side out. Press the edges flat. Hand stitch the opening closed. Push the lining into the bag through the zipper.

ice cream earbud bag......

FINISHED SIZE: 3″ × 6″

materials

- ⅓ yard of quilting cotton for ice cream and lining
- ¼ yard *or* 1 fat quarter of quilting cotton for cone
- ¼ yard each of 2 pom-pom trims
- 1 red wool ball 2 cm in diameter
- Fiberfill
- 18″ of 5 mm cord
- 1 cord stopper with 5 mm holes (OldSchoolGeekery on Etsy)
- 2 cord ends for 5 mm cords (*optional*)
- 1″ key ring
- 3″ of ⅓″-wide ribbon

cutting

ICE CREAM AND LINING

- 2 pieces using the Ice Cream Earbud Bag ice cream pattern (pullout page P2)

CONE

- 1 piece using the Ice Cream Earbud Bag ice-cream cone pattern (pullout page P2)
- 1 piece using the Ice Cream Earbud Bag ice-cream cone top pattern (pullout page P1)

instructions

Seam allowances are ¼″.

1. Fold the ice-cream cone in half, right sides together, aligning the edges. Sew down one straight side. **Fig. A**

2. Slip the ribbon through the key ring and fold the ribbon in half. Pin the ribbon tab to the top edge of the cone at the seam, with the ring facing inward. **Fig. B**

3. Pin the 2 trims around the outer edge of the cone so that they are facing inward. **Fig. C**

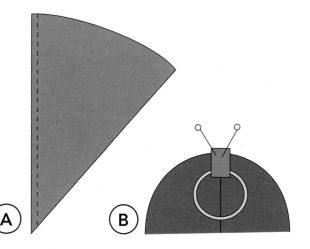

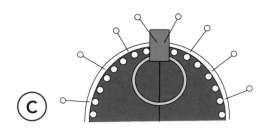

4. Pin the ice-cream cone top to the top of the cone, right sides together, with the trim in between. Sew around the entire outer edge, making sure to sew through all layers. *Fig. D*

5. Using scissors, carefully cut a slit approximately 1½″ long in the ice-cream cone top. Turn the cone right side out through the slit and fill with fiberfill. Set aside. (The cut will be hidden eventually.) *Fig. E*

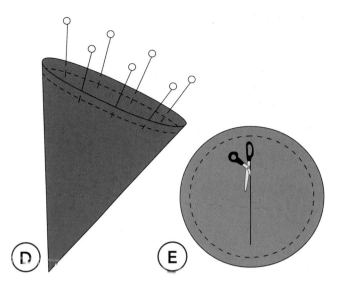

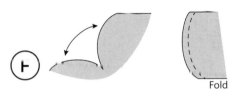

6. Sew the 4 darts on the 2 ice cream pieces. Do this by folding the V-shaped darts in half, right sides together. Line up the raw edges, pin, and sew. *Fig. F*

Fold

7. After the darts are sewn, turn the lining right side out and insert it into the ice cream piece, right sides together. Line up the stitched dart seams and pin together. Sew around the outside, leaving a 2½″ opening for turning. *Fig. G*

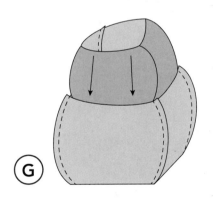

8. Every ½″, clip up to the seam around the outside edge. Turn the bag right side out and press. Hand stitch the opening closed, except for ¾″. (This is where the drawstring will eventually go.)

9. Topstitch ½″ from the edge all around the outside of the bag. *Fig. H*

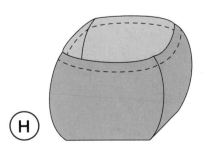

10. Using a safety pin or bodkin on one end of the cording, run the cord through the ½˝ channel sewn in Step 9. Slide the cord stop onto each end of the cord and either tie a knot or attach the cord ends. *Fig. I*

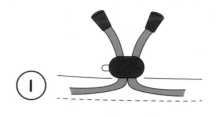

11. Using a needle and thread, hand stitch the bag onto the top center of the ice-cream cone. *Fig. J*

12. Sew the red felt ball to the top of the bag. Take care to avoid sewing it to the cording. *Fig. K*

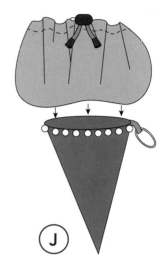

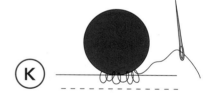

wraparound wallet

FINISHED SIZE: 3¾˝ × 4¾˝

materials

- ¼ yard of quilting cotton for wallet and pockets
- ⅛ yard of quilting cotton for star appliqué
- ¼ yard of lightweight fusible interfacing
- ¼ yard of medium-weight fusible interfacing
- 3″ × 3″ paper-backed fusible webbing
- 48″ of leather cord
- 4 assorted beads

cutting

WALLET AND POCKETS

- 2 pieces 5¼″ × 8½″ for wallet
- 2 pieces 5¼″ × 6″ for pockets

LIGHTWEIGHT FUSIBLE INTERFACING

- 2 pieces 2¾″ × 4¾″

MEDIUM-WEIGHT FUSIBLE INTERFACING

- 2 pieces 3¾″ × 4¾″

instructions

Seam allowances are ¼″.

1. Trace the Wraparound Wallet appliqué star (pattern pullout page P1) onto the paper side of the fusible web. Cut the star out approximately ¼″ outside the drawn line.

2. Lay the fusible web, paper side up, on the reverse side of the star fabric. Be sure the fabric is larger than the fusible web. To protect your iron, cover the fusible web with a nonstick pressing cloth. Follow the manufacturer's instructions to adhere your web to the fabric. Cut out on the drawn line and remove the paper backing.

3. Fold 1 wallet piece 5¼″ × 8½″ in half and lightly press to create a crease. Center the star in the middle of one of the sides and press to fuse the star to the fabric. Topstitch as desired. *Fig. A*

4. Fold a 5¼″ × 6″ pocket piece in half to make a rectangle that is 5¼″ × 3″, and press the fabric to create a crease. Open the fabric up again and place a piece of lightweight interfacing inside, aligning one edge along the crease. Press to adhere. Repeat with the other 5¼″ × 6″ pocket piece.

5. Referring to the diagram, place the 2 pockets from Step 4 onto the right side of the 5¼″ × 8½″ wallet piece without the star. The folds should be facing the center, and the raw edges should be aligned. Pin in place. *Fig. B*

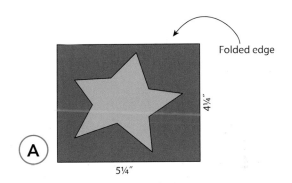

Folded edge

4¼″

5¼″

A

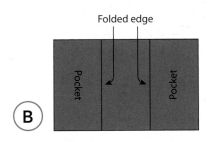

Folded edge

Pocket

Pocket

B

6. Fold the leather cord in half and tie a knot at the fold. Pin the cord to the middle of one short side of pocket unit, with the knot on the outside and the cord to the inside. *Fig. C*

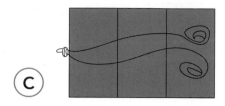

7. Lay the wallet piece with the star facedown on the pocket unit and pin. Sew around the outer edge, leaving an opening in the side opposite the knot for turning. *Fig. D*

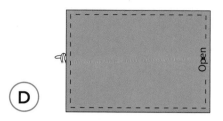

8. Clip the corners, turn right side out, and press. Slide a medium-weight fusible interfacing piece into one side of the wallet, all the way to the other edge. Slide the second one in, leaving a small gap between the 2 pieces for folding. Tuck the raw edges of the opening inward and press everything once more. Topstitch around the outside ⅛″ from the outer edge. Go across the middle a few times as well to help create a fold. *Fig. E*

9. Slide 2 beads onto each cord end and tie a knot to secure.

ladybug bag

FINISHED SIZE: 3½˝ wide × 3½˝ high × 2˝ deep

materials

- ⅛ yard of quilting cotton for outer shell
- ¼ yard of quilting cotton for lining and head
- ⅛ yard of tulle for wings
- ½ yard of ¼″-wide black velvet ribbon
- 6″ of mini pom-pom trim
- 5″ × 5″ black wool for spots
- 10″ × 10″ fusible fleece
- 5″ × 5″ paper-backed fusible webbing
- 5″ or longer zipper
- ¾″ nickel-plated swivel lever snap
- Black 6-strand embroidery floss

cutting

OUTER SHELL

- 2 pieces using the Ladybug Bag body pattern (pullout page P1)
- 1 piece 2¾″ × 8¾″ for bottom

LINING AND HEAD

- 2 pieces 1″ × 2″
- 2 pieces using the Ladybug Bag lining pattern (pullout page P1)
- 2 pieces 1½″ × 5″ for zipper strips
- 1 piece 2¾″ × 8¾″ for lining bottom
- 1 piece 2″ × 2″ for clip strap
- 2 pieces using the Ladybug Bag head pattern (pullout page P2)

WINGS

- 2 pieces 4″ × 4″

BLACK VELVET RIBBON

- 6 pieces 2″ long

FUSIBLE FLEECE

- 1 piece 2¼″ × 8¼″ for bottom
- 2 pieces 1″ × 4½″ for zipper strips
- 2 pieces using the Ladybug Bag lining pattern (pullout page P1)

instructions

Seam allowances are ¼˝.

1. Trace all 6 of the Ladybug Bag spot pattern (pullout page P1) onto the paper side of the fusible web.

2. Place the wool right side down on the ironing board. Place the fusible web, paper side up, on top of the wool. Be sure the wool is larger than the fusible web. To protect your iron, cover the fusible web with a nonstick pressing cloth. Follow the manufacturer's instructions to adhere your web to the wool. Cut out the spots on the drawn lines and remove the paper backing. Referring to the pattern piece, arrange all of the spots on the body, keeping them at least ¼˝ inside the edge. Iron in place. **Fig. A**

3. Using coordinating thread, stitch around the edges to secure the spots to the fabric. Use the buttonhole stitch if you are sewing by machine, or hand stitch. Using 3 strands of embroidery floss, stitch a straight line down the center of the ladybug. **Fig. B**

4. To make the clip strap, fold the 2 long sides in ¼˝ and press. Fold in half and press. Stitch down the sides to secure. Slide the strap through the clip, align the raw edges, and pin. **Fig. C**

5. Pin the clip strap in the middle of the back of the ladybug body. Pin the head onto the body, right sides together, with the clip strap in between. Sew across the top with a ¼˝ seam. **Fig. D**

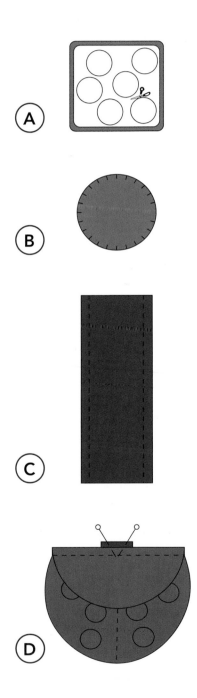

6. For the feet, fold the 6 pieces of 2″ ribbon in half and secure with a pin. Using the markings on the pattern piece, pin the ribbons to the back body piece with the loops facing in. Set aside. *Fig. E*

7. Fold each tulle piece in half and clip the corners to make rounded wings. *Fig. F*

8. Run a gathering stitch across the straight edge of the tulle and gather the 2 wings. Pin these along the top edge of the right side of the body. Pin the pom-pom trim on top of the wings. *Fig. G*

9. Pin and sew the head to the body, right sides together, along the straight side. Be sure to sew through all layers. Open and press, taking care not to melt the tulle with your iron. Set aside.

10. Start with a 1½″ × 5″ zipper strip right side up on your work surface. Place the zipper, teeth down, across the top of the fabric with the zipper centered. Pin in place, and sew using your zipper foot. *Fig. H*

11. Fold the fabric back from the zipper. Place the remaining side of the zipper face-down onto the right side of the remaining 1½″ × 5″ strip. Pin, and sew using your zipper foot. Press open. Topstitch down both sides of the zipper on the fabric. *Fig. I*

12. Pin the short ends of the zipper strip, with right sides facing, to the short ends of the outer shell bottom. Sew across, taking care when stitching over the zipper. *Fig. J*

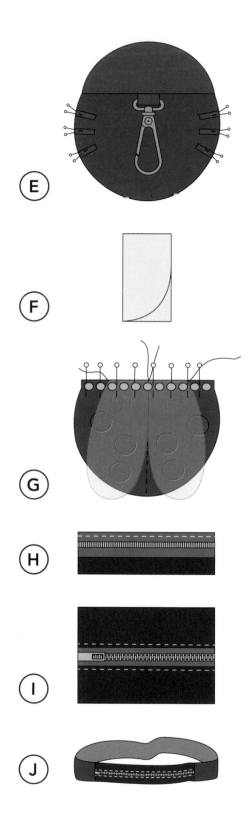

E

F

G

H

I

J

13. Unzip the zipper. With right sides facing, align and pin the seams of the zipper strip to the body. Be sure the head fabrics are aligned and the body fabrics are aligned. Sew all the way around, and repeat for the second side. Clip the edges well. Turn right side out.

14. Fold each of the lining zipper strips over ¼˝ on the longest side and press. Iron the fusible fleece interfacing to the corresponding lining fabric, sliding it under the fold. *Fig. K*

15. Place the 2 folded edges toward each other. Pin the 2 short ends of the zipper strip lining to the bottom lining with right sides together and sew. *Fig. L*

16. Sew the sides to the outer ring; clip the curves. Push the lining down into the bag. Arrange the zipper strips so they are on either side of the zipper. Hand stitch the lining into the bag, sewing along each side of the zipper. *Fig. M*

(K)

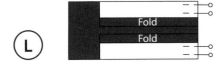

(L)

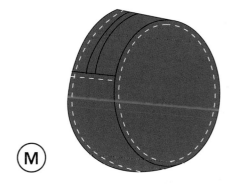

(M)

birdcage bag

FINISHED SIZE: 4″ wide × 4½″ high × 1½″ deep

materials

- ¼ yard of quilting cotton for outer shell
- ¼ yard of quilting cotton for lining
- 2½˝ × 2½˝ piece for bird body appliqué
- 2˝ × 2˝ piece for bird wing appliqué
- ⅛ yard of medium-weight fusible interfacing
- ⅛ yard of fusible fleece
- 6˝ × 6˝ paper-backed fusible webbing
- ¾˝ D-ring
- 12˝ zipper
- 1 yard of piping
- Yellow 6-strand embroidery floss

cutting

OUTER SHELL

- 2 pieces using the Birdcage Bag pattern (pullout page P2)
- 2 pieces 1˝ × 11¾˝ for zipper strips
- 1 piece 3˝ × 12˝ for strap
- 1 piece 3˝ × 3˝ for strap tab
- 1 piece 2˝ × 4¼˝ for bag bottom
- 2 pieces 2˝ × 2˝ for zipper tabs

LINING

- 2 pieces using the Birdcage Bag pattern (pullout page P2)
- 2 pieces 1¼˝ × 11¾˝ for zipper strips
- 1 piece 2˝ × 4¼˝ for bag bottom
- 2 pieces 2˝ × 2˝ for zipper tabs

MEDIUM-WEIGHT FUSIBLE INTERFACING

- 2 pieces 1˝ × 11¾˝ for zipper tabs
- 1 piece 2˝ × 4¼˝ for bag bottom
- 1 piece 2½˝ × 11½˝ for strap
- 1 piece 2½˝ × 2½˝ for strap tabs

FUSIBLE FLEECE

- 2 pieces using the Birdcage Bag pattern (pullout page P2)

instructions

Seam allowances are ¼˝.

1. Trace the Birdcage Bag appliqué patterns—bird, wing, beak, and swing (pullout page P1) onto the paper side of the fusible web.

2. Cut out the fusible web approximately ¼˝ outside the drawn line. Lay the fusible web shape on the reverse side of the appliqué fabric, paper side up. Be sure the fabric is larger than the fusible web shape. To protect your iron, cover the fusible web with a nonstick pressing cloth. Follow the manufacturer's instructions to adhere the web to the fabric. Repeat for each piece of the appliqué pattern. Cut out on the drawn lines and remove the paper backing. *Fig. A*

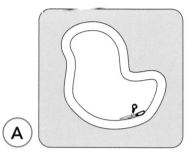

3. Arrange all of the pieces on the right side of the cage fabric and press to fuse.

4. Transfer the stitching design from the Birdcage Bag stitching guide (pattern pullout page P2) to the bag front. With a machine and black thread, stitch around the edge of the swing and bird to secure in place. Use a running stitch and 6 strands of floss to hand sew the cage bars.

5. Fuse the fusible fleece to the wrong side of both outer shell pieces, following the manufacturer's directions.

6. Iron the fusible interfacing for the strap to the center of the strap fabric. Fold the raw edges of the short ends over onto the interfacing and press. Fold the 2 remaining sides inward as well; press. Finally, fold the entire strap in half lengthwise. Topstitch around the entire outer edge of the strap. *Fig. B*

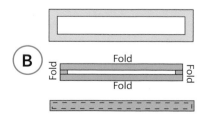

7. Slide the strap through the D-ring and fold one end over ½˝. Pin to hold. Take the remaining strap end, fold it over ½˝, and place it right up against the first strap end. Pin to secure. Sew a rectangle to secure the 2 straps; go over the stitches twice for stability. *Fig. C*

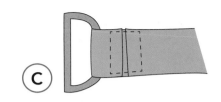

8. For the strap tab, fold 2 opposite sides in ¼˝ and press. Fold in half and press. Stitch down the sides to secure. Slide through the D-ring, aligning the raw edges, and pin. Set aside. *Fig. D*

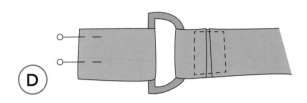

9. Fold and press each zipper tab in half. Place the right side of 1 tab on the teeth side of the zipper, just past the end of the teeth. Topstitch across. Using a ruler as a guide, place the raw edge of the second zipper tab at the 11¾˝ mark from the raw edge of the first tab. Pin on top of the zipper and sew across. Trim any excess zipper. *Fig. E*

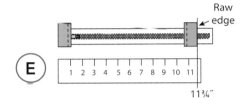

10. Start with a zipper strip right side up on your work surface. Place the zipper, teeth down, across the top of the fabric, with the zipper centered. Pin in place, and sew using your zipper foot. *Fig. F*

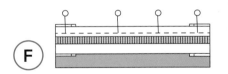

11. Fold the fabric back from the zipper. Place the other side of the zipper facedown onto the right side of the remaining zipper strip. Pin, and sew using your zipper foot. Press open. Topstitch down both sides of the zipper on the fabric. *Fig. G*

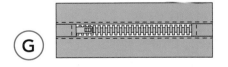

12. Pin the short ends of the zipper strip to the short ends of the outer shell bottom. Sew across these to form a ring. *Fig. H*

13. Pin the piping around both edges of the outer shell, raw edges aligned and with the cording side facing in. Pin the strap tab to the back of the outer shell at the top center, facing inward. Leave the raw edges of the strap tab ¼″ beyond the zipper strip's raw edges. *Fig. I*

14. Pin the zipper strip and bottom to the bag's side. Sew around the outer edge. Repeat for the second side. Be sure to have the zipper open during this step. *Fig. J*

15. Fold each of the lining zipper strips over ¼″ and press, sliding the zipper strip interfacing under the fold. Iron the interfacing to the corresponding lining fabrics.

16. Place the 2 folded edges toward the middle. Align the raw edges of the zipper tabs with the raw edges of the lining strip (with the fold facing in) and pin. Place the remaining strip on the other corner. Sew across the tab to connect all 3 pieces. Repeat for the second side. *Fig. K*

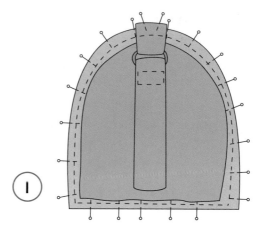

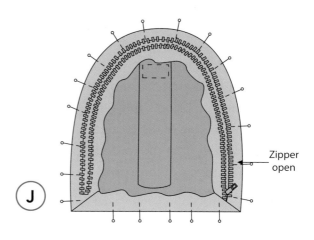

Zipper open

17. Sew the 2 short ends of the zipper strip lining to the bottom lining. *Fig. L*

18. Sew the bag lining sides to the outer ring. Clip the curves. Push the lining down into the bag. Arrange the zipper strips so that they are on either side of the zipper. Hand stitch the lining to the bag. *Fig. M*

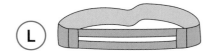

Back side of zipper

Lining

whale coin purse

FINISHED SIZE: 4˝ × 7˝

materials

- ¼ yard of quilting cotton or light twill for outer shell
- ¼ yard of denim or twill for lining
- 7″ zipper
- Black 6-strand embroidery floss

cutting

OUTER SHELL

- 2 pieces using the Whale Coin Purse body pattern (pullout page P2)
- 1 piece using the Whale Coin Purse bottom pattern (pullout page P2)
- 1 piece using the Whale Coin Purse tail pattern (pullout page P2)
- 2 pieces using the Whale Coin Purse fin pattern (pullout page P1)

LINING

- 2 pieces using the Whale Coin Purse body pattern (pullout page P2)
- 1 piece using the Whale Coin Purse bottom pattern (pullout page P2)
- 1 piece using the Whale Coin Purse tail pattern (pullout page P2)
- 2 pieces using the Whale Coin Purse fin pattern (pullout page P1)

 note

Cut fins and tails as a set. Place the outer shell and lining fabrics right sides together to cut each set.

instructions

Seam allowances are ¼˝.

1. Using 6 strands of floss, add eyes by sewing a French knot on each of the whale body pieces, using the pattern as a guide. Sew the mouth using a running stitch. *Fig. A*

2. Place an outer shell and lining fin piece together, right sides facing. Stitch around the edge, leaving the one indicated side open for turning. Clip and turn. Repeat for the second fin and the tail pieces. *Fig. B*

3. Tuck the raw edges of the fin inward and press. Hand stitch a fin to each side of the whale's outer body, using the pattern for placement. *Fig. C*

4. Start with an outer shell piece right side up on your work surface. Place the zipper, teeth down, across the top of the fabric, using the pattern piece for placement. Pin in place along the curve of the body. *Fig. D*

5. Place a piece of lining fabric, right side down, on top of the pinned zipper. Make sure to match the top and side edges of the outer shell and lining. Pin the lining in place. *Fig. E*

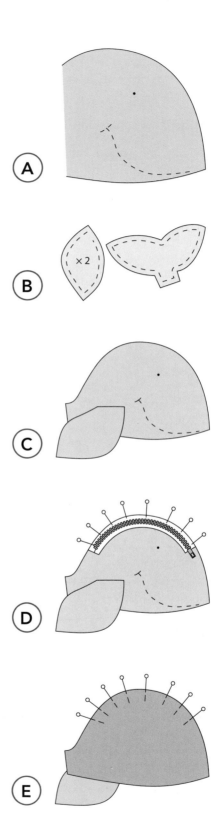

6. Sew the zipper only, using the zipper foot on your machine. *Fig. F*

7. Fold the fabric back from the zipper so that the outer shell and lining are wrong sides together. Place the remaining side of the zipper facedown on the right side of the remaining outer shell piece. Align the outer shell sides with the fabrics sewn in Step 6. Pin in place. Place the remaining lining fabric, right side down, on the pinned zipper. Sew the zipper only, using the zipper foot on your machine.

8. Arrange and pin the right sides of the outer shell fabrics together. Pin together the 2 lining pieces. Sew each side together, taking care to leave the tail and bottom areas unsewn. Fold the tail in half and place the fold facing the top of the body. Align the raw edges and pin. Sew. *Fig. G*

9. Pin the bottom of the whale to the bottom of the outer shell, right sides together, and sew around it entirely.

10. Working only with the lining, place the lining bodies right sides together and sew from each end of the zipper. Pin the lining bottom to the whale's body. Sew around the lining, leaving a 2˝ opening for turning. *Fig. H*

11. Clip the curves and turn right side out. Hand stitch the opening closed. Push the lining into the bag through the zipper.

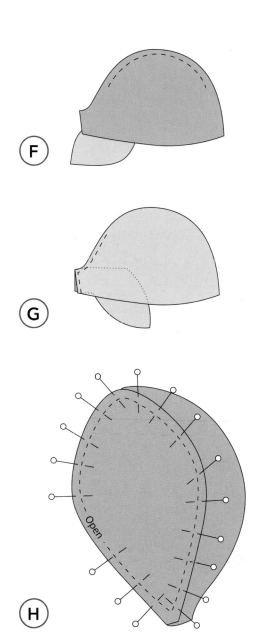

Open

small wallet

FINISHED SIZE: 3½″ × 6½″

materials

- ¼ yard of quilting cotton for outer shell, lining 1, and lining 2
- ¼ yard of quilting cotton for pocket and sides
- ⅛ yard of quilting cotton for zipper pouch and zipper tab
- 3″ × 6″ red felt
- 1 yard of piping
- 1 button approximately ¾″ in diameter
- ¾″ D-ring
- ¾″ × 1″ spring clasp
- 6″ zipper
- Magnetic snap
- ¼ yard of medium-weight fusible interfacing
- ⅛ yard of heavyweight fusible interfacing (such as fast2fuse HEAVY Interfacing by C&T Publishing) for strap and button tab
- ¼ yard of batting

cutting

OUTER SHELL

- 2 pieces (1 for outer shell and 1 for lining) using the Small Wallet outer shell pattern (pullout page P2)
- 1 piece 2″ × 2″ for D-ring tab
- 1 piece 3″ × 12″ for strap

LINING 1 POCKETS AND SIDES

- 2 pieces using the Small Wallet pockets pattern (pullout page P2)
- 4 pieces using the Small Wallet side pattern (pullout page P1)

LINING 2 ZIPPER POUCH AND BUTTON TAB

- 4 pieces 3½″ × 5″ for zipper pouch
- 2 pieces 1½″ × 2″ for zipper tabs
- 2 pieces using the Small Wallet button tab pattern (pullout page P1)

FELT

- 1 piece using the Small Wallet scallop pattern (pullout page P1)

MEDIUM-WEIGHT FUSIBLE INTERFACING

- 1 piece using the Small Wallet pockets pattern (pullout page P2)

- 1 piece using the Small Wallet outer shell pattern (pullout page P2)
- 2 pieces 3½″ × 5″ for zipper pouch

HEAVYWEIGHT FUSIBLE INTERFACING

- 1 piece 1½″ × 11½″ for strap
- 1 piece using the Small Wallet button tab pattern (pullout page P1)

BATTING

- 1 piece using the Small Wallet outer shell pattern (pullout page P2)

instructions

Seam allowances are ¼˝.

1. Following the manufacturer's instructions, fuse the interfacing to the reverse side of 1 button tab, 1 pocket, 1 outer shell, and 2 zipper pouch linings. Transfer the snap markings to the corresponding pieces as well. Attach the magnetic snaps to those markings. Note that the snap on the outer piece should be placed on the piece with the interfacing for extra support. *Fig. A*

2. Place the 2 pocket pieces right sides together and stitch along the top and the bottom. Turn and press. *Fig. B*

3. Lay the pocket from Step 2 on the outer shell piece without the snap. Pin in place. Stitch down the middle of the wallet, securing the bottom of the pocket, and set aside. *Fig. C*

4. Place the 2 side pieces right sides together. Sew along the top and the bottom, turn, and press. Fold in half and press again. Set aside. *Fig. D*

5. Fold a zipper tab in ¼˝ on each of the 1½˝ sides. Press and fold in half. Press again and set aside. Repeat with the second tab.

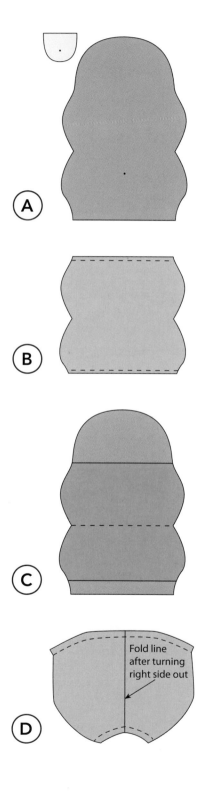

Fold line after turning right side out

6. Slide the zipper tab over one end of the zipper. Pin in place and sew across. Trim the remaining side of the zipper so the end of the tab will be at the end of the zipper pouch. Slide the tab on and sew across. *Fig. E*

7. Start with a zipper pouch piece right side up on your work surface. Place the zipper, teeth down, across the long side of the fabric. Pin in place. *Fig. F*

8. Place another zipper pouch piece, right side down, on top of the pinned zipper. Make sure to match the top and side edges of the 2 fabrics. Pin in place. *Fig. G*

9. Sew using the zipper foot on your machine. *Fig. H*

10. Fold the fabric back from the zipper so that the fabrics are wrong sides together. Place the remaining side of the zipper facedown on the right side of another zipper pouch piece. Align the outer edges with the edge of the zipper. Pin in place.

11. Place the last zipper pouch piece, right side down, on top of the zipper. Align the zipper's edge. Pin and sew in place.

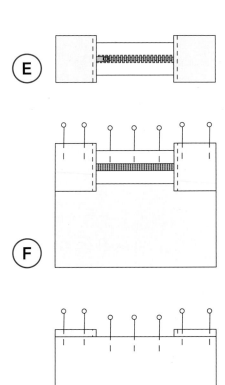

E

F

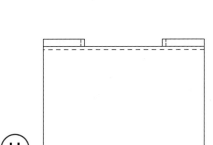

G

H

12. Arrange and pin the right sides of the outer zipper pouch together. Arrange and pin the right sides of the inner pouch together. Fold the zipper tabs so the fold is facing the outer shell. Sew across the longer sides of the zipper pouch only. Turn right side out and press. *Fig. I*

13. Place each side of the zipper pocket into the fold of the side pieces. Stitch down each side to secure. *Fig. J*

14. Starting on one side of the wallet, align all raw edges. There will be several layers: the side piece, pocket, and wallet lining. Pin. Sew 2 securing seams ⅛″ from the raw edge, 1 on each side of the folded center. Repeat for the other side of the wallet. *Fig. K*

15. Find the top center of the lining and the middle of the felt scallop, and mark with a pin. Align the marks and pin the scallop to the top center of the lining. Continue pinning each side of the felt. *Fig. L*

16. Place the button tab pieces right sides together and sew around the curved edge. Clip, turn, and press. *Fig. M*

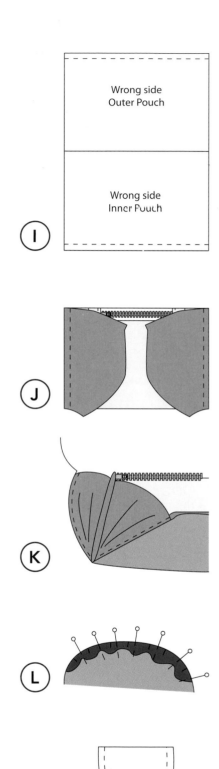

17. Pin the button tab, with the magnet side down, to the center—on top of the felt scallop.

18. Fold the raw edges of the D-ring tab in ¼″ on opposite sides, press, and then fold in half. Sew down the sides. *Fig. N*

19. Slide the D-ring tab through the D-ring and fold in half. Pin to secure. Place the D-ring tab on the right side of the lining where indicated on the pattern, with the D-ring facing inward. *Fig. O*

20. Pin the piping all the way around the other outer piece (the one with the magnet), aligning the raw edges and with the cord facing in. Sew the piping to the outer piece. *Fig. P*

21. Pin and sew the 2 outer shells together, right sides facing, except for the straight edge. *Fig. Q*

TIP: Pin and sew sections together instead of the entire wallet at once.

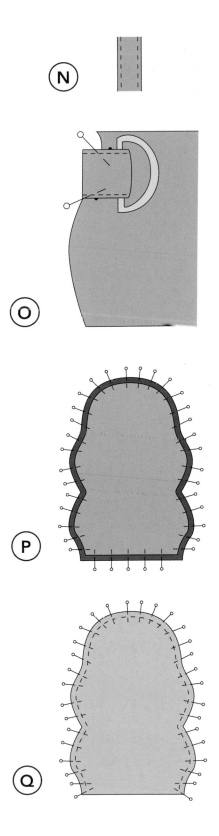

22. Clip the curves and turn right side out. Hand stitch the opening closed.

23. Iron the fusible interfacing to the center of the strap fabric. Fold the short ends over onto the interfacing and press. Fold the 2 long sides inward and press. Finally, fold the entire strap in half lengthwise. Topstitch around the entire outer edge of the strap, using a ⅛˝ seam allowance. *Figs. R–T*

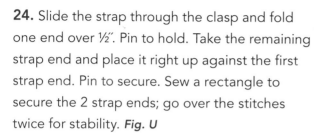

24. Slide the strap through the clasp and fold one end over ½˝. Pin to hold. Take the remaining strap end and place it right up against the first strap end. Pin to secure. Sew a rectangle to secure the 2 strap ends; go over the stitches twice for stability. *Fig. U*

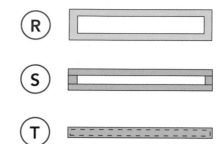

25. Hand stitch the button to the front of the tab.

drawstring house bag

FINISHED SIZE: 3˝ wide × 5˝ high × 3˝ deep

materials

- ⅓ yard of linen or quilting cotton for house base
- ⅛ yard of quilting cotton for roof
- ⅛ yard of quilting cotton for lining and door
- ⅛ yard of quilting cotton for windows
- 3 assorted 1″ × 1″ wool pieces for flowers
- 2″ × 4″ green wool for leaves
- ⅛ yard of heavyweight craft interfacing (Peltex)
- 2″ × 2″ medium-weight fusible interfacing
- 8 grommets with ¼″-diameter holes
- 3″ × 3″ paper-backed fusible webbing
- ½ yard of 5 mm cording
- 2 beads approximately 15 mm, with a 5 mm hole

cutting

HOUSE BASE

- 1 piece using the Drawstring House Bag pattern (pullout page P2)

ROOF

- 2 pieces 4¼″ × 14″

LINING

- 1 piece using the Drawstring House Bag pattern (pullout page P2)

HEAVYWEIGHT CRAFT INTERFACING (PELTEX)

- 2 pieces 3″ × 2½″
- 4 pieces 2¼″ × 2½″
- 1 piece 2½″ × 2½″

MEDIUM-WEIGHT FUSIBLE INTERFACING

- 4 pieces 1″ × 1″

WOOL

- 3 flowers using the Drawstring House Bag flower pattern (pullout page P1)
- 2 leaves using the Drawstring House Bag leaves pattern (pullout page P1)

instructions

Seam allowances are ¼˝.

1. Trace the Drawstring House Bag door and window appliqué patterns (pullout page P1) onto the paper side of the fusible web.

2. Cut out the fusible web approximately ¼˝ outside the drawn line. Place the appliqué fabric, right side down, on the ironing board. Place the fusible web on top of the fabric, paper side up. Be sure the fabric is larger than the fusible web. To protect your iron, cover the fusible web with a nonstick pressing cloth. Follow the manufacturer's instructions to adhere your web to the fabric. Repeat for each piece of the appliqué patterns. Cut the pieces out on the drawn line and remove the paper backing. Arrange the pieces on the outer shell piece, keeping them at least ¼˝ inside the edge. Iron in place. *Fig. A*

3. Using coordinating thread, topstitch around the edges to secure the fabric. *Fig. B*

4. Iron the Peltex to the walls and floor of the house. *Fig. C*

5. Pin the right sides of the house walls together. Sew the 4 sides of the house base. Repeat this step for the lining base. *Fig. D*

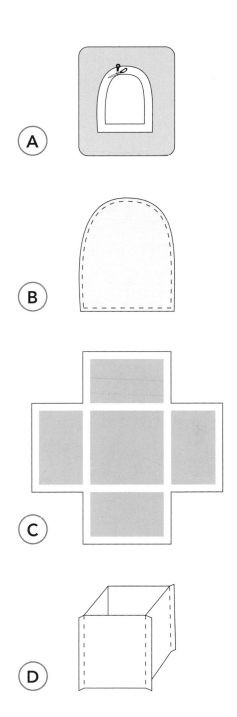

6. Lay the outer roof fabric on your work surface with the wrong side up. Place a ruler along the top edge. Measure ¾˝ in from the left side and place the edge of the Peltex for the roof, fusible side down, along this line. Place the second edge of the roof at 7½˝ from the edge. Referring to the illustration, place the medium-weight interfacing pieces at 4¼˝, 6¼˝, 11˝, and 13˝, with the fusible side down. Iron these all in place. *Fig. E*

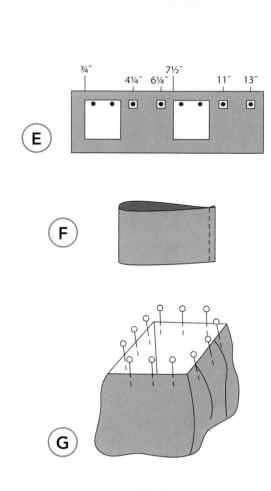

7. Flip the fabric over. Referring to figure E, place a mark ½˝ down from the top in the center of the interfacing. Mark ½˝ down and ½˝ in on each side of the Peltex roof pieces as well. This is where the grommets will eventually be attached.

8. Align the 2 short sides of the roof, right sides together. Pin and sew. Repeat this step for the roof lining piece. *Fig. F*

9. Find the center of the roof by folding and marking it with a pin. Pin the seam of the roof to one of the back corners of the house. Pin the center, which you marked with a pin, to the opposite corner of the house. Pin the rest of the roof around the walls of the house. There will be a slight gather in the roof when pinning it on the house; keep the gathers at the front and back of the house. Sew around to join the roof and the house. *Fig. G*

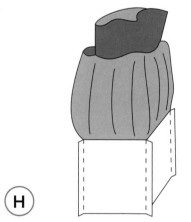

10. Repeat Step 9 with the roof lining and house lining.

11. Turn the lining right side out and push it down into the house so that right sides are facing. *Fig. H*

12. Align the 2 top edges of the roof and pin. Sew around the top, leaving a 3″ gap for turning. Turn right side out and press the top seam. Hand stitch the opening closed.

13. Press the top of the roof seam. Following the manufacturer's instructions, add grommets at the 8 marks that were previously placed on the roof (Step 7).

14. Thread the cording through the 2 front grommets, the sides, and then out the back. When the cord is pulled, the roof should fold like an accordion. Tie a bow to secure. Add beads to the end of the cord and tie a knot to secure. *Fig. I*

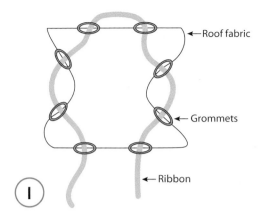

← Roof fabric

← Grommets

← Ribbon

I

stand-up flower pouch

FINISHED SIZE: 5˝ wide × 6˝ high × 3˝ deep

·····materials

- ¼ yard of quilting cotton for flap and back

- ¼ yard of quilting cotton for front and outer bottom

- ¼ yard of quilting cotton for lining

- ¼ yard of batting

- Scraps of various fabrics for flower petals, stem, and flower center appliqué

- 4″ × 4″ paper-backed fusible webbing

- 3″ × 3″ felt in 2 different colors for flower center

- 1 magnetic snap

- Orange 6-strand embroidery floss

cutting ·····

FLAP AND BACK

- 1 piece 6″ × 6½″

- 1 piece using the Stand-Up Flower Pouch flap pattern (pullout page P1)

FRONT AND OUTER BOTTOM

- 1 piece 6″ × 6½″

- 1 piece using the Stand-Up Flower Pouch bottom pattern (pullout page P2)

LINING

- 2 pieces 6″ × 6½″

- 1 piece using the Stand-Up Flower Pouch flap pattern (pullout page P1)

- 1 piece using the Stand-Up Flower Pouch bottom pattern (pullout page P2)

BATTING

- 2 pieces 6″ × 6½″

- 1 piece using the Stand-Up flower Pouch flap pattern (pullout page P1)

- 1 piece using the Stand-Up Flower Pouch Bottom pattern (pullout page P2)

FLOWER PETALS

- 7 flower petal sets using the Stand-Up Flower Pouch petal pattern (pullout page P1)

STEM

- 1 piece ¾″ × 6″

FLOWER CENTER APPLIQUÉ

- 1 piece using the Stand-Up Flower Pouch flower center appliqué pattern (pullout page P1)

FLOWER CENTER

- 1 piece using the Stand-Up Flower Pouch medium center pattern (pullout page P1)

- 1 piece using the Stand-Up Flower Pouch small center pattern (pullout page P1)

instructions

Seam allowances are ¼˝.

1. Place the stem down the middle of the front piece and stitch. ***Fig. A***

2. Attach the magnetic snap, centered 1˝ from the bottom of the flap and 3¼˝ down in the center of the bag front. ***Fig. B***

3. Align the batting pieces with the corresponding outer fabric pieces. Place the front and back pieces right sides together and sew down each side. Repeat this step for the lining (excluding the batting). ***Fig. C***

4. Pin the outer bottom piece to the outer front and back, right sides together, aligning the points with the side seams. Sew. Repeat this step for the lining. ***Fig. D***

5. Turn the outer piece right side out and push it into the lining. Align the side seams and pin. Sew across the top edge of the front 2 pieces only. Turn right side out and push the lining into the bag. ***Fig. E***

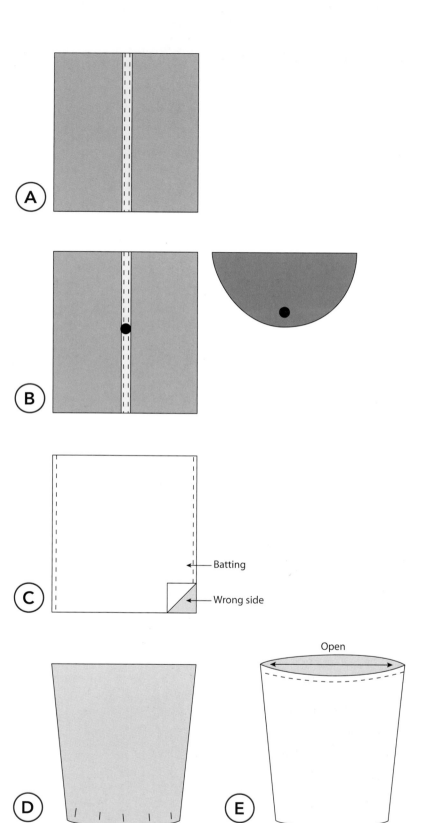

6. Place the right sides of the flap together and sew around the outer curved edge, leaving the straight edge unsewn. Clip the curves and turn right side out. *Fig. F*

7. Turn the opening on the bag's edge under ¼″ and press. Slide the raw edges of the flap into the opening, making sure that the magnetic snap is facing the correct way and that it aligns with the other part of the snap. *Fig. G*

8. Carefully topstitch across the back, and set aside.

9. Trace the Stand-Up Flower Pouch appliqué patterns (pullout page P1) onto the paper side of the fusible web. Cut out the fusible web approximately ¼″ outside the drawn line. Iron the webbing to the reverse side of the flower center appliqué and cut out on the drawn line. Peel the paper backing off and set aside.

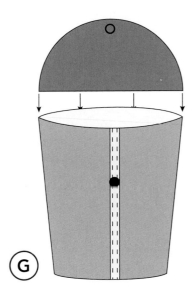

10. Pin the individual flower petals right sides together and sew around the curved edge. Clip, turn, and press. *Fig. H*

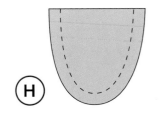

11. On your work surface, arrange and pin the petals approximately ¼″ under the edge of the flower center. *Using an ⅛″ seam allowance*, sew around the outer edge of the circle to secure the petals. *Fig. I*

12. Trim the edges of the felt ovals with scalloped or pinking shears. Stitch the 2 felt ovals to the center of the flower using the orange 6-strand embroidery floss.

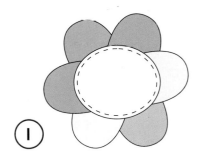

13. Arrange the flower on the flap and iron in place. Taking care to not sew the magnet, sew around the center once more.

ruffled brush bag

FINISHED SIZE: 3½˝ high × 8½˝ wide × 3¾˝ deep

materials

- ⅛ yard of quilting cotton for top and tabs
- ¼ yard of quilting cotton for lining and side
- ¼ yard of quilting cotton for center
- ¼ yard of medium-weight fusible interfacing
- 1 yard of piping

- 1 yard of ¼″-wide velvet ribbon
- 1 yard of ⅓″-wide gingham ribbon
- 2″ of 1″-wide velvet ribbon
- 8″ zipper
- ¾″ D-ring

cutting

TOP AND TABS

- 2 pieces using the Ruffled Brush Bag top pattern (pullout page P1)
- 2 pieces 1½″ × 2½″ for zipper tabs
- 1 piece 2″ × 2″ for D-ring tab

LINING AND SIDE

- 2 pieces using the Ruffled Brush Bag pattern (pullout page P1)
- 4 pieces using Ruffled Brush Bag side pattern (pullout page P1)

CENTER

- 2 pieces 6¼″ × 5″
- 2 pieces 9″ × 5″

MEDIUM-WEIGHT FUSIBLE INTERFACING

- 2 pieces using the Ruffled Brush Bag pattern (pullout page P1)

instructions

Seam allowances are ¼″.

1. Run a gathering stitch across the top and the bottom of the 9″ × 5″ rectangle (the 9″ sides). Pull and gather to 6¼″, wrong sides together, and pin all 4 sides to the 6¼″ × 5″ rectangle. Repeat for the second set of center pieces. *Fig. A*

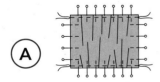

2. Align the top edge of the sides with the top edge of the ruffled square. With right sides together, pin and sew all the way down the sides. Open the sides out and press. Repeat with the remaining center and sides. *Fig. B*

3. Cut 2″ of ¼″-wide velvet ribbon. Pin it, as well as the 1″-wide velvet ribbon piece, to a side on the front ruffled portion. (This is making the ribbon decoration that is on the front of the bag.) Pin the piping along the top, matching the raw edges. Place the bag top, right side down, on the piping and pin, again matching raw edges. Sew along this edge. Place the remaining bag top, right side down, on the second center-and-sides piece. Sew along this edge. *Fig. C*

4. For the D-ring tab, fold and press the 2″ × 2″ square in half. Open it back up and fold the raw edges to the fold. Press and fold in half again. Sew down the sides to secure. *Fig. D*

5. Slide on the D-ring and fold the tab in half. Pin the tab just above the piping on the left side of the bag front, with the D-ring facing inward. *Fig. E*

6. Fold each of the short sides of the 1½″ × 2½″ zipper tabs in ¼″ and press. Fold the tabs in half.

7. Place one of the tabs over one end of the zipper and stitch across. Be sure that the zipper pull is closed; then trim the zipper to 8½″. Place the remaining tab over the cut end and stitch. Be sure that the zipper plus the tabs measures at least, if not exactly, 9¼″. *Fig. F*

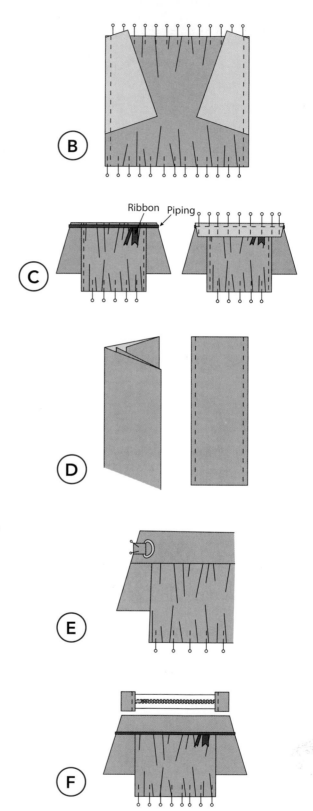

8. Start with an outer shell piece right side up on your work surface. Place the zipper, teeth down, across the top of the fabric with the zipper centered. Pin in place. *Fig. G*

9. Place a piece of lining fabric right side down on top of the pinned zipper. Make sure to match the top and side edges of the outer shell and lining. Pin the lining in place. *Fig. H*

10. Sew using the zipper foot on your machine. *Fig. I*

11. Fold the fabric back from the zipper so that the outer shell and lining are wrong sides together. Place the remaining side of the zipper facedown on the right side of the remaining outer shell piece. Align the outer shell fabric sides with the fabrics sewn in Step 10. Pin in place.

12. Place the lining right side down on top of the zipper. Make sure to match the top and side edges of the outer shell and lining fabrics. Pin and sew the second zipper side in place. Before proceeding, partially open the zipper.

13. Arrange and pin the right sides of the outer fabric together and the lining together. Fold the zipper tabs so the fold is facing the outer shell of the fabric. Sew around the outer edges, leaving approximately a 3″ gap for turning along the bottom of the lining and the notched corners unsewn. *Fig. J*

14. To form the corners, open the notched corners. Match the lining side seams and bottom seams at 1 corner. Pin together and sew. Sew all 4 corners this way.

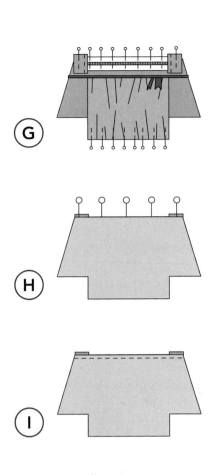

G

H

I

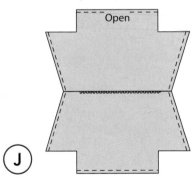

Open

J

15. Turn right side out. Hand stitch the opening closed. Push the lining into the bag.

16. Tie a bow and sew it onto the bag just above the ribbons. Clip the ends of the 2 velvet ribbons to form a V-shaped notch. *Fig. K*

17. Using the velvet and gingham ribbons, fold the ribbons in half to make a loop. Send the loop through the ring. Send the ends of the ribbons through the loop. Trim the ribbons to desired length.

bangle wristlet

FINISHED SIZE: 4″ × 6″ (bag only)

materials

- ¼ yard of quilting cotton for outer shell
- ¼ yard of cotton for lining
- ⅛ yard of faux leather
- 7″ zipper (or longer)
- Bangle bracelet
- 1″ O-ring that opens with screws (buckleguy.com)
- 2″ or 3″ tassel
- Double-sided quilter's tape (sold in the quilters' section for holding seams until stitched)

cutting

OUTER SHELL

- 2 pieces 5½″ × 7½″
- 2 pieces 1½″ × 3″ for zipper tabs

LINING

- 2 pieces 5½″ × 7½″

FAUX LEATHER

- 2 pieces 2½″ × 5½″
- 1 piece using the Bangle Wristlet pattern (pullout page P2)

instructions

Seam allowances are ¼″.

1. Align a faux leather piece along the bottom of the outer shell. To avoid pinning the leather, double-sided tape may be used to secure it to the fabric. Topstitch along the edge. Repeat this step for the second piece. *Fig. A*

2. Find the center of the front outer piece on the opposite side from the leather. Tape the leather strap, right side facing up, at the center. *Fig. B*

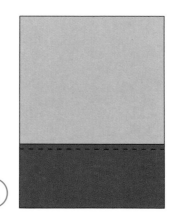

(A)

(B)

3. Fold each of the short ends of the zipper tabs in ¼˝ and press. Fold in half.

4. Place a zipper tab over one end of the zipper and stitch across. Making sure that the zipper is closed first, trim the zipper to 6½˝. Place the other tab over the cut end of the zipper and stitch. Be sure that the zipper plus the tabs measure at least, if not exactly, 7½˝. *Fig. C*

5. Start with an outer shell piece right side up on your work surface. Place the zipper, teeth down, along the side of the fabric, with the zipper centered. Pin in place. *Fig. D*

6. Place a piece of lining fabric right side down on top of the pinned zipper. Make sure to match the top and bottom edges of the outer shell and the lining. Pin the lining in place, taking care to pin the faux leather only in the seam allowance. *Fig. E*

7. Sew using the zipper foot on your machine. *Fig. F*

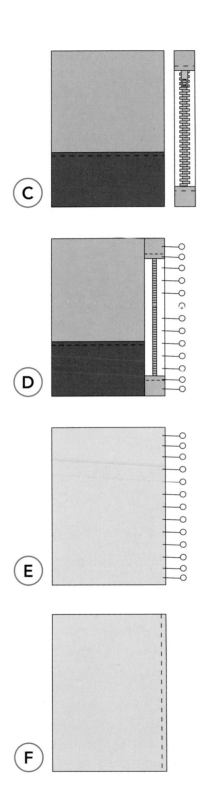

8. Fold the fabric back from the zipper so that the outer shell and lining are wrong sides together. Place the remaining outer shell right side down, facing the zipper. Align the outer shell fabric sides with the fabrics sewn in Step 7. Pin in place. *Fig. G*

9. Flip the pieces over, and place the lining right side down on top of the zipper. Make sure to match the top and bottom edges of the outer shell and lining fabrics. Pin and sew in place.

10. Arrange the outer shell pieces right sides together and the lining pieces right sides together. Fold the zipper tabs so that the fold is facing the outer shell of the fabric. Sew around the outer edge, leaving approximately a 3″ gap on the long side of the lining for turning. *Fig. H*

11. Clip the corners and turn right side out. Press the edges flat. Hand stitch the opening closed. Push the lining into the bag.

12. Fold the skinny end of the leather tab back under the larger end of the tab, leaving a loop large enough for the O-ring to slide through later. Secure with a piece of double-sided tape. *Fig. I*

13. Send the strap through the bangle and place the O-ring tab on the pouch. Secure with double-sided tape. Topstitch across both tab ends to secure to the pouch. *Fig. J*

14. Open the O-ring and slide the tassel onto it. Then send the O-ring through the loop. Screw closed.

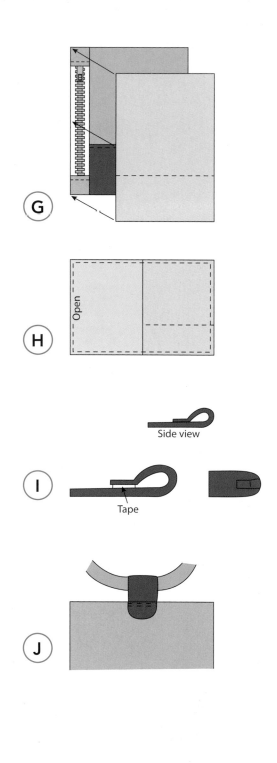

journaling wallet

FINISHED SIZE: 6˝ wide × 9˝ long × 2½˝ deep

materials

- ¼ yard of quilting cotton for outer shell and middle angled pocket

- 3 assorted ¼ yards *or* 1 fat quarter of quilting cotton for large and small angled pockets, back tab, and straight paper pocket

- ⅓ yard of quilting cotton for washi pocket and binding fabric

- ¼ yard of quilting cotton for lining and sides

- 5 pieces 3″ × 4″ each of assorted quilting cottons for appliqué

- ¼ yard of fusible fleece

- ⅛ yard of paper-backed fusible webbing

- 22″ zipper

- 10″ of fold-over elastic

- ¼ yard of kraft•tex (by C&T Publishing)

- ½ yard each of 2 different ribbons (your choice of width)

- ½ yard of mini pom-pom trim

cutting

OUTER SHELL AND MIDDLE ANGLED PENCIL POCKET

- 2 pieces 5½″ × 9″

- 2 pieces 5½″ wide × 7½″ high (small side 4½″)

LARGE ANGLED PEN POCKET AND BACK TAB

- 2 pieces 5½″ wide × 8⅞″ high (small side 6⅛″)

- 2 pieces 3″ × 8½″

SMALL ANGLED PAPER POCKET

- 2 pieces 5½″ wide × 4″ high (small side 1″)

STRAIGHT PAPER POCKET

- 1 piece 7″ × 9″

TIP: To cut angled pockets, place rectangles right sides together, with the 5½″ side at the bottom. Mark the small side measurement up from one corner. Cut from the mark across to the upper corner.

WASHI POCKET

- 1 piece 5½″ × 10½″

- 2 pieces 2½″ × width for binding

LINING AND SIDES

- 2 pieces 5½″ × 9″ for lining

- 4 pieces 1¼″ × 22″ for zipper sides

FUSIBLE FLEECE

- 2 pieces 5½″ × 9″

- 2 pieces 1″ × 22″

FOLD-OVER ELASTIC

- 1 piece 2″ long

- 1 piece 8″ long

KRAFT•TEX

- 2 pieces 4¾″ × 8″

instructions

Seam allowances are ¼″.

1. Trace the Journaling Wallet happy appliqué patterns (pullout page P2) onto the paper side of the fusible web. *Fig. A*

2. Cut out the fusible web approximately ¼″ outside the drawn line. Place the appliqué fabric right side down on the ironing board; place the fusible web paper side up on top of the fabric. Be sure the fabric is larger than the fusible web. To protect your iron, cover the fusible web with a nonstick pressing cloth. Follow the manufacturer's instructions to adhere the web to the fabric. Repeat for each letter of the appliqué pattern. Cut out on the drawn line and remove the paper backing.

3. Arrange the letters on the right side of a 5½″ × 9″ outer shell piece, keeping them at least ½″ inside the outer edge. Iron in place.

4. Topstitch around the edges to secure the fabric, using thread in the color of your choice. Referring to the photo, sew the trim pieces across the bottom of the fabric. Set aside.

5. Fold the washi pocket in half. Sew a strip of elastic pulled snugly across the fold. *Fig. B*

6. Fold the straight paper pocket in half and topstitch along the edge, ⅛″ in from fold.

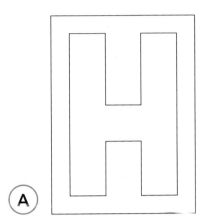

A

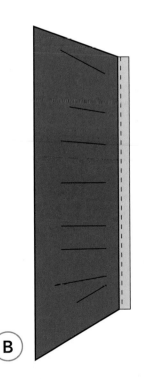

B

7. Place the right sides of the small angled pockets together with the mini pom-pom trim layered between. Sew along the top edge. Turn, press, and topstitch ⅛″ from the edge. Sew the medium and large pockets together in the same manner. Turn, press, and topstitch ⅛″ from the slanted edge. Topstitch the ribbon in place on the medium pocket. *Fig. C*

8. Place the fleece, fusible side up, on your work surface. Center the kraft•tex on top of the fleece. *Fig. D*

Add 1 lining piece faceup on top of the kraft•tex. Iron to fuse the fleece to the edges of the fabric. Repeat for both lining fabrics.

9. Arrange the 3 pockets on the front of the lining. Align and pin the raw edges together. When pinning on the washi pocket, pin the sides first and then pin along bottom, where the fabric will be slightly gathered. *Fig. E*

10. Iron the fusible fleece to the 2 lining strips 22″ long, aligning the edges on one long side. *Fig. F*

Place 1 outer strip and 1 lining strip (the side without fleece) together, with the zipper between the layers. Stitch the zipper in place.

11. Flip the fabric so it faces outward; press. Topstitch. Repeat for the second side. *Fig. G*

12. Sandwich one end of the zipper strip in between the 2 back tab pieces, with the right sides of the fabric facing the zipper. Sew, turn, and press. Topstitch, taking care to lift the needle over the zipper. *Fig. H*

13. Repeat for the second side, creating a circular band. Set aside.

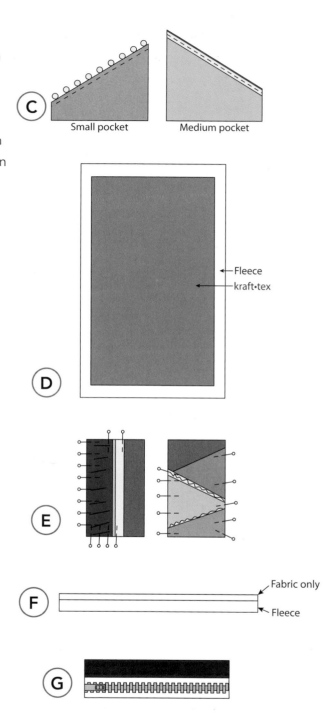

C
Small pocket   Medium pocket

D
Fleece
kraft•tex

E

F
Fabric only
Fleece

G

H

14. Sew the short ends of the binding together; press. Then press the entire length of binding in half lengthwise.

15. Find the center of the back tab and mark it with a pin. Find the center of the zipper side and mark it with a pin as well. Find the center of each side between the 2 pins and mark them with a pin. *Fig. I*

16. On all 4 sides, find the center of the cover and mark it with a pin, as in Step 15. *Fig. J*

17. Align the sides to the right side of the cover, lining up the pins. Be sure the zipper teeth and pull are facing outward and that the zipper is starting at the top left of the cover. Pin or clip the sides to the outer edge of the cover.

18. Go back and pin or clip the binding to the top of the raw edges. At this point you may find it easier to use wonder clips instead of pins. *Fig. K*

19. Sew around the outer edge of the sandwich. Go slowly, and if you don't have dual feed, you might have to pull a little to get it through.

20. Repeat for the second side. Unzipping the zipper will help with this cumbersome step.

21. Hand stitch the binding around the raw edges.

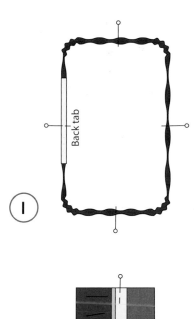

I

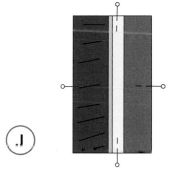

J

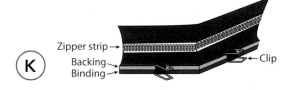

K

wallet clutch·············

FINISHED SIZE: 5″ × 9″

materials

- ⅓ yard wool or wool blend for outer shell
- ⅓ yard each of 3 different quilting cottons for lining and pocket
- 9″ zipper
- 2″ of ¼″-wide elastic
- 2 sew-on leather snap fasteners 1″ × 3″ (3DANsupplies on Etsy)
- ⅓ yard of heavyweight woven interfacing
- ⅔ yard of medium-weight woven fusible interfacing
- All-purpose sewing thread to match strap color
- 10″ of ribbon approximately ¾″ wide
- 8″ × 8″ paper-backed fusible webbing
- 2 pieces 2″ × 2″ for toadstool cap and stem

cutting

OUTER SHELL

- 2 pieces 1¾″ × 13″
- 1 piece 7¼″ × 13″

LINING 1

- 1 piece 9½″ × 13″
- 1 piece 6½″ × 9½″ for credit-card pocket

LINING 2

- 2 pieces 1½″ × 13″ for side straps
- 1 piece 3″ × 5¾″ for handle
- 1 piece 7½″ × 9½″ for checkbook pocket
- 1 piece 9½″ × 9½″ for cash pocket
- 1 piece 5″ × 9½″ for credit-card pocket
- 2 pieces 1″ × 2½″ for zipper tabs

LINING 3

- 2 pieces 5″ × 9½″ for zipper pocket

HEAVYWEIGHT WOVEN INTERFACING

- 1 piece 9½″ × 13″
- 1 piece 1¼″ × 5¾″

MEDIUM-WEIGHT WOVEN FUSIBLE INTERFACING

- 1 piece 6½″ × 9½″ for credit-card pocket
- 1 piece 7½″ × 9½″ for checkbook pocket
- 1 piece 9½″ × 9½″ for cash pocket
- 1 piece 5″ × 9½″ for credit-card pocket

instructions

Seam allowances are ¼˝.

1. Place the 9½˝ × 13˝ piece of lining fabric faceup on work surface. Measure 5½˝ from the bottom edge up and mark with a pin on each side. Draw a line from pin to pin. This marks the center of the wallet. **Fig. A**

2. Iron the corresponding interfacing onto the back of the checkbook pocket. Fold the checkbook pocket in half, to 3¾˝ × 9½˝, and press. Align the raw edges along the marked centerline, with the folded side facing the *bottom*. **Fig. B**

3. Iron the corresponding interfacing onto the back of the cash pocket. Fold the cash pocket in half, to 4¾˝ × 9½˝, and press. Align the raw edges along the centerline, with the fold facing the *top*. Draw a line across the cash pocket 2½˝ down from the fold and stitch along this line. **Fig. C**

4. Iron the corresponding interfacing onto the back of the credit-card pockets. Fold the credit-card pockets (lining 1 and lining 2) in half to create a 3¼˝ × 9½˝ and a 2½˝ × 9½˝ rectangle. Press.

5. Trace the Wallet Clutch toadstool appliqué pattern (pullout page P1). Arrange and fuse it to the bottom of the smaller credit-card pocket, ¼˝ from the top fold and 1˝ in from the raw edge. Hand stitch around the outside of each piece, using a contrasting thread. Be sure to stitch *only* through the front credit-card pocket.

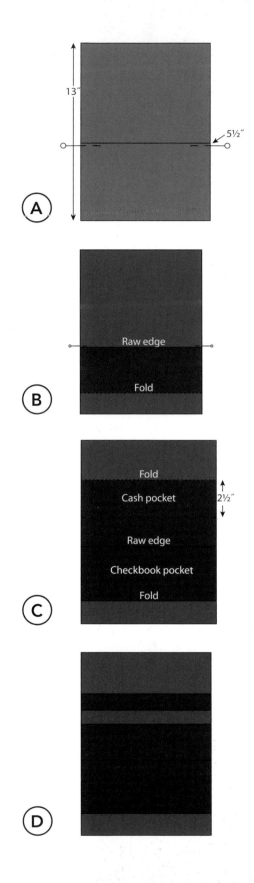

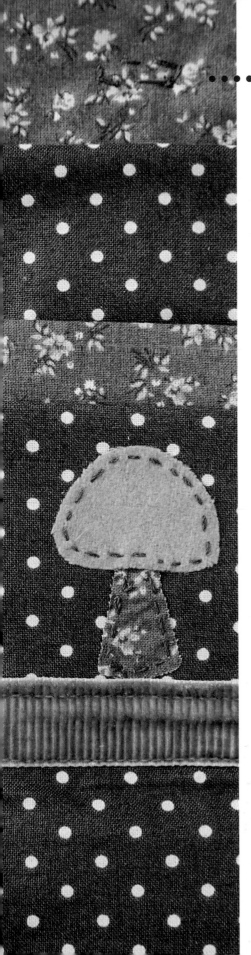

6. Layer these pockets on top of the cash pocket, with raw edges at the centerline of the wallet. *Fig. D*

7. Find the center of the credit-card pockets and secure with a pin. Flip the lining out of the way. Stitch approximately 1″ down just on the front of the cash pocket and the credit-card pockets until you reach the bottom stitching line for the cash pocket. Arrange the credit-card pockets so they are flat on the lining and stitch the remaining centerline, sewing through all of the layers.

8. Baste down the sides, using an ⅛″ seam allowance to secure the pocket edges to the shell. *Fig. F*

9. Roll the 2″ of elastic into a circle. Overlap the raw ends and sew the elastic loop onto the lining just above the checkbook pocket.

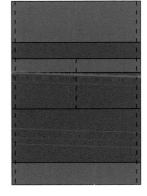

10. Place a ribbon over the raw edges at the centerline. Let the raw edges of the ribbon hang off each side of the wallet. Topstitch around the edges of the ribbon.

11. Fold the 3″ × 5¾″ handle fabric in half lengthwise. Place the interfacing into the fold. Fold in the raw edges of the longer sides and press. Topstitch each side at ⅛″.

12. Pin the wrong side of the side straps to the right side of the larger outer shell fabric piece. On top, add the right side of the shorter outer shell fabric. Align the raw edges of the 3 fabrics and pin. Sew down each side. *Fig. F*

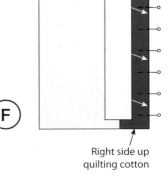

Right side up quilting cotton

13. Press the seam open. Fold the remaining raw edge of the strap under ¼″ and press. Measure 3½″ from the bottom edge; this is where the handle strap goes. Tuck the short sides of the handle under the folded side straps and pin. Topstitch down each side of the straps to secure. *Fig. G*

TIP : The handle will not lie flat so that a hand can slide in to hold it. At this point you can adjust how much space you want under the handle.

14. Fold a zipper tab ¼″ in on each side of the 1½″ sides. Press and fold in half. Press again. Repeat with the second tab. Slide a zipper tab over one end of the zipper. Pin in place and sew across. Trim the remaining side of the zipper so the end of the tab will be at the end of the outer shell. Slide on the tab and sew across. *Fig. H*

15. Start with the outer shell piece right side up on your work surface. Place the zipper, teeth down, across the handle side of the fabric, with the zipper centered. Pin in place. *Fig. I*

16. Place a zipper pocket piece right side down on top of the pinned zipper. Make sure to match the top and side edges of the outer shell and zipper pocket piece. Pin in place. *Fig. J*

17. Sew using the zipper foot on your machine. *Fig. K*

18. Fold the fabric back from the zipper so that the outer shell and zipper pocket are wrong sides together. Place the remaining side of the zipper facedown on the right side of the lining piece with the checkbook pocket closest to the zipper. Pin in place.

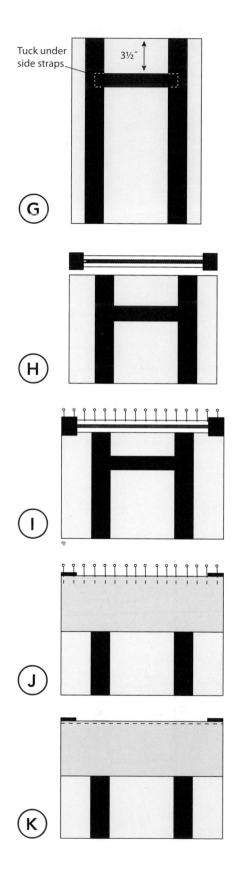

Tuck under side straps

3½″

G

H

I

J

K

19. Place the remaining zipper pocket right side down on top of the zipper. Make sure to match the top and side edges of the outer shell lining fabrics. Pin, and sew in place.

20. Arrange and pin together the right sides of the outer fabric to the inner fabric and the pocket pieces. Starting at the pocket, sew around the outside of the wallet clutch, leaving approximately a 4″ gap along the zipper pocket side for turning. *Fig. L*

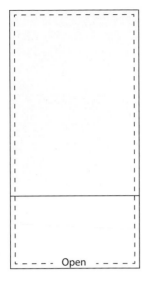

21. Clip the corners and turn the wallet right side out. Press the edges flat. Hand stitch the pocket opening closed. Push in through the zipper.

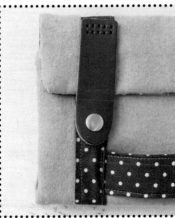

22. Arrange the leather snap fasteners on the front of the wallet. Hand stitch into place, taking care to sew *only* through the outer fabric.

log jewelry roll ··········

FINISHED SIZE: 4″ × 8″ rolled up; 8″ × 15″ open

materials

- ⅓ yard of quilting cotton with tree-bark design for outer shell
- ½ yard of linen or quilting cotton for lining
- ⅛ yard of quilting cotton for log ends
- ⅛ yard of quilting cotton for pocket flaps
- 2 zippers 8″ long (1 log color, 1 flap color)
- 1 yard of suede cord
- ⅝ yard of piping
- Brown 6-strand embroidery floss
- 5 sew-on snaps
- 5 buttons ¾″–1″ wide
- 8¼″ × 8¼″ ByAnnie's Soft and Stable
- 8¾″ × 14½″ batting

cutting

OUTER SHELL

- 2 pieces 4⅝″ × 8¾″ for outer log ends
- 1 piece 8¾″ × 14½″ for log wrap
- 1 piece 2″ × 8″ for connector
- 2 pieces 1½″ × 3″ for zipper tabs

LINING

- 1 piece 8¾″ × 8¾″ for log lining
- 2 pieces using the Log Jewelry Roll log end pattern (pullout page P2)
- 1 piece 8¾″ × 13″ for log wrap lining
- 1 piece 2″ × 8¾″ for log wrap lining
- 1 piece 8¾″ × 10¾″ for zipper pocket

- 1 piece 8½″ × 13½″ for pocket strip
- 1 piece 6½″ × 13½″ for pocket strip
- 2 sets of 2 leaves each using the Log Jewelry Roll leaf pattern (pullout page P1)

LOG ENDS

- 2 pieces 6″ × 6″

POCKET FLAPS AND ZIPPER TABS

- 4 pieces using the Log Jewelry Roll large flap pattern (pullout page P2)
- 6 pieces using the Log Jewelry Roll small flap pattern (pullout page P2)
- 2 pieces 1½″ × 3″ for zipper tabs

instructions

Seam allowances are ¼˝.

1. Trace the log end pattern and tree rings onto the 2 log end pieces using the Log Jewelry Roll log end pattern (pullout page P2). Embroider the rings onto each end, using 6 strands of floss and a running stitch. After stitching, cut out the log end pieces. *Fig. A*

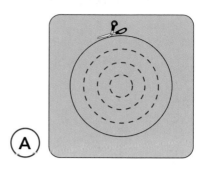

2. Stitch the 5 sets of pocket flaps, right sides together. Clip, turn, and press. Topstitch approximately ⅛˝ from the edge around the curved sides. *Fig. B*

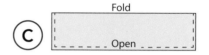

3. Fold the 2 pocket strips in half, with right sides facing inward. Press. Sew around the outer raw edge, leaving a 3˝ opening for turning. Clip the corners, turn, and press. Set the pockets aside. *Fig. C*

4. Fold the 2˝ × 8˝ connector strip in half lengthwise, with the right sides facing outward. Press. *Fig. D*

5. Center the strip along one raw edge of an outer log piece, with right sides facing. Place the remaining outer log on top, with the right side facing the strip, and pin in place. Sew across. *Fig. E*

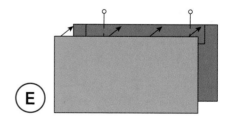

6. Fold the zipper tabs by turning in ¼˝ on each of the short sides. Press. Fold the tab in half and press. Repeat this step for all 4 tabs. Set the 2 lining tabs aside.

7. Place a zipper tab over one end of the zipper; stitch across. Making sure that the zipper pull is in, trim the zipper to 7½˝. Place the tab over the cut end and stitch. Be sure that the zipper plus the tabs measure at least, if not exactly, 8¾˝. *Fig. F*

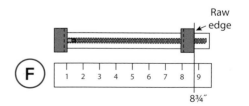

8. Start with one end of an outer shell piece right side up on your work surface. Place the zipper, teeth down, across the top of the fabric with the zipper centered. Pin in place.

9. Sew using the zipper foot for your machine. *Fig. G*

10. Place the remaining side of the zipper face-down on the right side of the remaining side of the outer log shell piece. Sew along this side.

11. Pin and sew the piping and log ends to each end of the shell. Clip the curved edges and turn right side out. *Fig. H*

12. Place the right sides of the lining together. Sew 1″ in on each side. *Fig. I*

13. Sew each log end lining piece to the lining. Clip the curved edges.

14. Roll the Soft and Stable piece and place it into the log so that the edges align with the zipper. Place the lining into the log as well. Arrange so that the lining opening and the zipper line up. Hand stitch the folded edge of the lining to the back of the zipper. *Fig. J*

15. Place a lining tab over one end of the second zipper, and stitch across. Making sure the zipper pull is in, trim the zipper to 7″. Place the remaining lining tab over the cut end and stitch. Be sure that the zipper plus the tabs measure at least, if not exactly, 8¾″.

16. Fold the zipper pocket in half to make an 8¾″ × 5⅜″ rectangle. Press. Place the folded side just over the edge of the zipper tape and pin in place. Topstitch ⅛″ from the fold. *Fig. K*

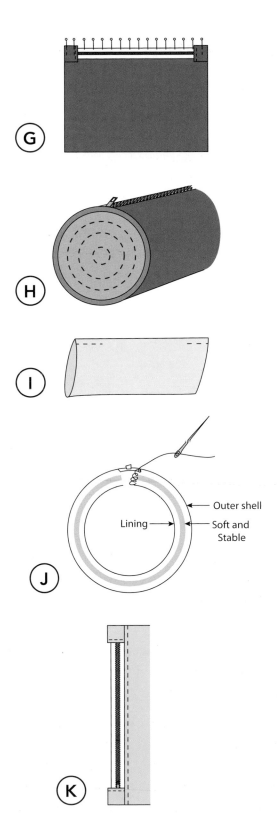

G

H

I

Outer shell

Lining

Soft and Stable

J

K

17. Align the 3 raw edges of the pocket to the larger piece of the log wrap lining; pin in place. *Fig. L*

18. Place the raw edges of the 3 small flaps across the bottom of the small lining piece. The center pocket should align with the center of the strip. Each side pocket should start ¾″ in from the raw edge. *Fig. M*

Place the small strip, flaps included, right side down on the lining top. Sew all the layers together. Open and press back the small lining piece.

19. Place the lining right side down on top of the outer fabric. Fold the wrap in half lengthwise and trim off the top corners to create a curve. *Fig. N*

20. Unfold the wrap pieces and place on top of the batting; trim the batting to match the curves at the top as well. Fold the suede cord in half and center it at the top between the lining and outer shell fabrics, with the ends hanging inward. Sew all 3 layers together, leaving the bottom open. Turn the piece and press. *Fig. O*

21. Pin the remaining side of the zipper tape to the outer wrap to keep it in place.

22. Fold the large pocket in half to find the center. Find the center of the outer wrap as well. Pin the center of the large pocket to the center of the outer wrap. The bottom of the pocket needs to be on top of the zipper tape. Sew down the center of the pocket. Pin each side to the side of the wrap and stitch in place. *Fig. P*

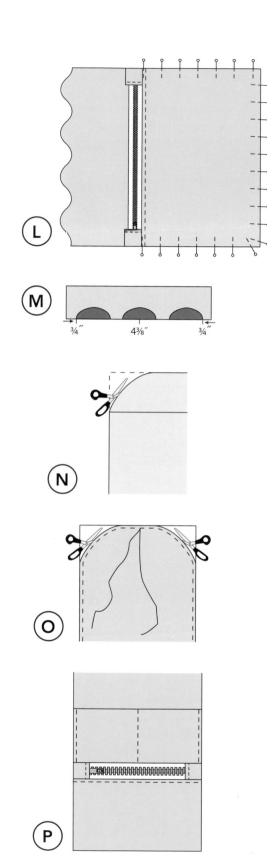

23. Accordion-fold a ½˝ gather on each side. This should make the pocket lie flat on the wrap; gather more or less as necessary to get the pocket flat. Pin in place. Repeat this step for the second pocket. Sew along the bottom of the pocket, making sure to catch the top zipper tape as well as the bottom of the pockets. *Fig. Q*

24. Measure 4½˝ from the top edge and draw a line across. Place the raw edges of the 2 large flaps on that line above each of the pockets. Pin in place. *Fig. R*

25. Measure 4¼˝ in from each side of the small pockets and place a mark. Then measure 2⅝˝ in from each side on the wrap and place a mark. Align the markings on the pockets to the wrap. Follow Steps 22–24 to create the 3-pocket row. This time, be sure to catch the top of the large flaps instead of the zipper tape.

26. Fold the raw edge of the wrap bottom in approximately ¼˝ and press. Slide this end onto the strip coming from the bottom of the log. Pin to secure. Stitch along the bottom to secure all of the layers. *Fig. S*

27. Place a set of leaves right sides together. Stitch around, leaving an opening for turning. Clip the curves and turn right side out. Tie a knot on each end of the suede. Place the leaves over the knots through the opening. Hand stitch the opening closed. *Fig. T*

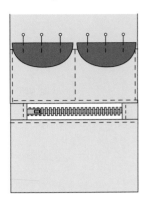
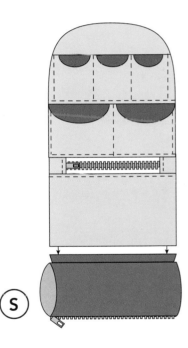
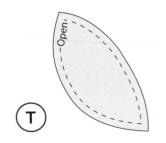

28. Sew the 5 sets of sew-on snaps to the pockets and flaps, and sew a button onto the front of each flap.

clear zipper pouch

FINISHED SIZE: 7″ × 9″

materials

- ⅓ yard of quilting cotton for outer shell
- ⅓ yard of Premium Clear Vinyl (by C&T Publishing)
- ⅓ yard of quilting cotton for lining
- 9″ zipper
- 2″ O-ring (buckleguy.com)
- Glitter, photos, and so on to place under the vinyl
- ¼″ double-sided quilter's tape (sold in the quilters' section for holding seams until stitched)
- Assorted ribbons

cutting

OUTER SHELL
- 2 pieces 7½″ × 9½″

VINYL
- 2 pieces 7½″ × 9½″

LINING
- 2 pieces 7½″ × 9½″
- 2 pieces 1½″ × 2½″ for zipper tabs
- 1 piece 2″ × 2″ for strap

instructions

Seam allowances are ¼″.

1. Place the double-sided tape on 3 sides of each of the outer fabric pieces. Peel the paper side of the tape off and carefully position the vinyl on top so that the edges are lined up. Press down to secure. **Fig. A**

2. Slide photos, glitter, and other items in between the fabric and the vinyl. The side to be seen should be next to the vinyl.

TIP The glitter will most likely want to stick to the vinyl—use this to your advantage to spread it out and get it where you would like it on the bag.

3. Topstitch around all 4 sides to secure the contents. Topstitch in rows lengthwise across the piece. These 2 pieces will now be referred to as the outer shell pieces. *Fig. B*

4. Fold each of the short ends of the zipper tabs in ¼″ and press. Fold in half. Place a zipper tab over the end of the zipper and sew across. Making sure the zipper is closed, trim the remaining side of the zipper so the end of the tab will be at the end of the zipper pouch. Slide the tab on and sew across. *Fig. C*

5. Start with an outer shell piece right side up on your work surface. Place the zipper, teeth down, across the top of the fabric with the zipper centered. Pin in place. *Fig. D*

6. Place a piece of lining fabric right side down on top of the pinned zipper. Make sure to match the top and side edges of the outer shell and lining. Pin the lining in place. *Fig. E*

7. Sew using the zipper foot on your machine. *Fig. F*

8. Fold the fabric back from the zipper so that the outer shell and lining are wrong sides together. Place the remaining side of the zipper facedown on the right side of the remaining outer shell piece. Align outer shell fabric sides with the fabrics sewn in Step 7. Pin in place.

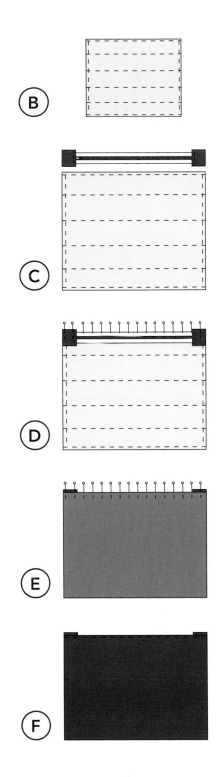

9. Fold the strap piece ¼″ in on each long side and press. Fold in half and press again. Stitch along each long side. Slide on the O-ring and fold the strap in half. Pin 1″ down from the zipper with the ring facing inward. *Fig. G*

10. Arrange and pin the right sides of the outer shell together and the lining fabric together. Sew around the outside of the pouch, leaving approximately a 3″ gap for turning along the bottom of the lining. *Fig. H*

11. Clip the corners and turn right side out. Press the edges flat. Hand stitch the opening closed. Push into the bag.

12. Fold ribbons in half to make a loop. Send the loop through the ring. Send the ends of the ribbons through the loop. Trim to the desired length.

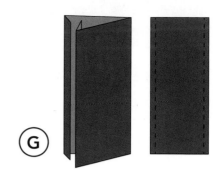

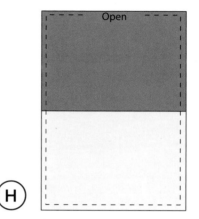

tablet bag

FINISHED SIZE: 8″ × 10″

materials

- ⅓ yard of quilting cotton for outer shell

- ⅓ yard of quilting cotton for lining and notebook pocket

- ¼ yard of quilting cotton for elastic pocket

- Fat quarter of quilting cotton for handles

- ⅛ yard of quilting cotton for flower embellishment

- ⅓ yard of ByAnnie's Soft and Stable

- ¼ yard of medium-weight woven fusible interfacing

- ⅛ yard of two-sided heavyweight fusible interfacing (such as fast2fuse HEAVY Interfacing by C&T Publishing)

- 7 assorted ribbons and trims approximately 14″ in length

- ½ yard of 2 bias tapes

- ½ yard of mini pom-pom trim

- 10″ of ¾″-wide elastic

- 4″ × 2″ green felt

cutting

OUTER SHELL

- 2 pieces 8½″ × 10½″ for front and back

- 2 pieces 8½″ × 1½″ for bag sides

- 1 piece 10½″ × 1½″ for bag bottom

LINING AND NOTEBOOK POCKET

- 2 pieces 8½″ × 10½″ for front and back

- 2 pieces 8½″ × 1½″ for bag sides

- 1 piece 10½″ × 1½″ for bag bottom

- 2 pieces 6¾″ × 10½″ for notebook pocket

ELASTIC POCKET

- 1 piece 6½″ × 14″

HANDLES

- 4 pieces using the Tablet Bag handle pattern (pullout page P2)

FLOWER EMBELLISHMENT

- 1 piece 1½″ × 22″

SOFT AND STABLE

- 2 pieces 8½″ × 10½″ for front and back

- 2 pieces 8½″ × 1½″ for bag sides

- 1 piece 10½″ × 1½″ for bag bottom

MEDIUM-WEIGHT WOVEN FUSIBLE INTERFACING

- 1 piece 6¾″ × 10½″ for notebook pocket

TWO-SIDED HEAVYWEIGHT FUSIBLE INTERFACING

- 2 pieces using the Tablet Bag handle pattern (pullout page P2)

FELT

- 1 piece using the Tablet Bag leaf pattern (pullout page P1)

instructions

Seam allowances are ¼˝.

1. Sew 3 trim pieces across the top of the front, approximately ¾˝ from the top edge. *Fig. A*

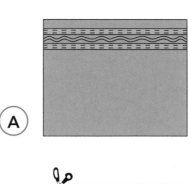

2. Fold the 2 notebook pocket pieces in half and use the Tablet Bag pocket pattern (pullout page P2) to cut the curve of the pocket. Cut a curve into the woven interfacing as well. *Fig. B*

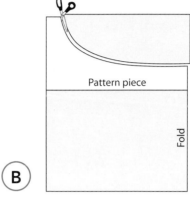

3. Iron the woven interfacing to the back of one of the pocket pieces. Arrange the 2 pieces so that the right sides are facing outward. Pin a piece of bias tape across the top edge, making sure it hangs off 1˝ on each side. Tuck the mini pom-pom trim under the bias tape and sew along the edge. *Fig. C*

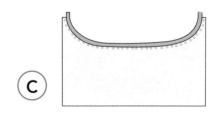

4. Fold the elastic pocket in half lengthwise and press. Arrange and sew 2 trims across the pocket ¾˝ from the fold. (You are creating the pocket for the elastic.) *Fig. D*

5. Thread 10˝ of elastic through the channel. When the back end reaches the end of the tube, stop pushing it through and sew across that end to secure the elastic in place. Continue threading the elastic until you reach the opposite side. Stitch the front end to secure it in place. *Fig. E*

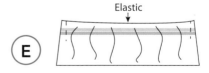

6. Find the center of the elastic pocket. With the elastic gathered, it will be at 5¼˝ at the top, while at the bottom it will be at 7˝. Mark each center with a pin. Find the middle of the notebook pocket and stitch a seam down the elastic pocket onto the notebook pocket. *Fig. F*

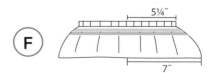

7. Pin the 3 sides of the elastic pocket to the notebook pocket. There will be a slight gather in the bottom when you pin. Pin the pockets to the front of the bag. *Fig. G*

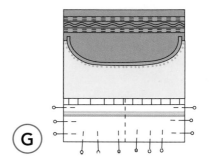

8. Place 2 handle pieces right sides together and sew along the top curve. Repeat this step with the second set of handle pieces. *Fig. H*

9. Clip the curves and turn the handles right side out. Push the fast2fuse handle piece up into each handle, really working to get it all the way to the seam. Press with an iron to hold it in place. Pin the bias tape across the bottom curve of each handle and sew along the tape edge to secure it. *Fig. I*

10. Place the Soft and Stable pieces on the corresponding outer pieces. Sew the 2 bag sides to the bag bottom along the short ends. Repeat this step for the lining. *Fig. J*

11. Right sides together, align the bag side/bottom unit with the corresponding sides of the front outer shell. Sew each seam. Sew the remaining edge to the back outer shell. Repeat this step for the lining pieces, but leave a 5˝ opening along the bottom for turning later. *Fig. K*

Bag side   Bag bottom   Bag side

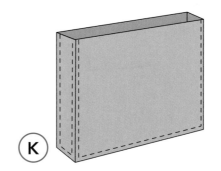

12. On the outer bag, measure 1¼˝ in from each side seam and place a mark. The handles will go between these 2 marks. Pin the handles to each side of the bag, matching raw edges and with the handles facing inward. *Fig. L*

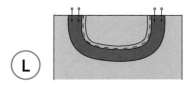

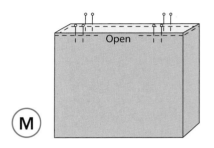

13. Turn the lining so that the right sides are out. Push the lining down into the bag and pin the top edge, aligning the side seams. *Fig. M*

14. Sew around the top edge through all layers.

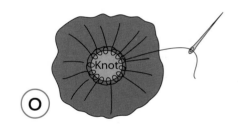

15. Turn right side out and hand stitch the opening in the lining closed. Push the lining into the bag.

16. Fold the flower fabric strip in half lengthwise and press. Tie a knot at one end. *Fig. N*

17. With a needle and thread, run a gathering stitch along the raw edge of the flower strip, starting just past the knot. Pull snug and arrange the raw edge snugly around the knot to form a circle. Stitch the raw edge to the knot. *Fig. O*

18. Stitch the flower and both 4˝-long ribbons to the felt leaf. Arrange and stitch the flower just under the handle on the front of the bag.

beach purse

FINISHED SIZE: 9" × 11"

materials

- ⅓ yard of linen or linen blend for outer shell

- ⅓ yard of quilting cotton for lining

- ¼ yard or 1 fat quarter of quilting cotton for pink flamingo appliqué

- 4″ × 4″ quilting cotton for orange starfish appliqué

- ¼ yard or 1 fat quarter of quilting cotton for green leaves appliqué

- 4″ × 4″ quilting cotton for turquoise fish appliqué

- ⅛ yard or 1 fat quarter for blue water appliqué

- 4″ × 4″ quilting cotton for yellow-green flamingo legs and beak appliqué

- 1½″ × 1½″ quilting cotton for black flamingo beak appliqué

- ¼ yard of quilting cotton for straps and tabs

- 1 yard of piping

- ⅓ yard of medium-weight woven fusible interfacing

- ¼ yard of heavyweight fusible interfacing

- 8″ zipper

- 2 natural brass ¾″ D-rings

- 2 natural brass ¾″ swivel trigger snap clips (buckleguy.com)

- 1 natural brass ¾″ double loop

- ½ yard of paper-backed fusible webbing

- 2 black ⅛″ buttons

cutting

OUTER SHELL

- 2 pieces 9″ × 12″ for front and back

- 2 pieces 1½″ × 3″ for zipper tab

LINING

- 2 pieces 9″ × 12″ for front and back

- 1 piece 6½″ × 11″ for inside pocket

STRAPS AND TABS

- 1 piece 3″ × 42″ for strap

- 1 piece 3″ × 12″ for strap

- 2 pieces 3″ × 4″ for tabs

MEDIUM-WEIGHT WOVEN FUSIBLE INTERFACING

- 2 pieces 9″ × 12″ for front and back

- 1 piece 5½″ × 6½″ for inside pocket

HEAVYWEIGHT FUSIBLE INTERFACING

- 2 pieces 1½″ × 3½″ for tabs

- 1 piece 1½″ × 53½″ for strap

instructions

Seam allowances are ¼˝.

1. Trace the Beach Purse appliqué patterns (pullout pages P1 and P2) onto the paper side of the paper-backed fusible web.

2. Cut out the fusible web approximately ¼˝ outside the drawn line. Place the appliqué fabric right side down on the ironing board. Place the fusible web, paper side up, on the fabric. Be sure that the fabric is larger than the fusible web. To protect your iron, cover the fusible web with a nonstick pressing cloth. Follow the manufacturer's instructions to adhere the webbing to the fabric. Repeat this step for each piece of the appliqué pattern. Cut out each piece on the drawn line and remove paper backing. Arrange all pieces on an outer shell piece, keeping them at least ¼˝ inside the edge. Iron in place. *Fig. A*

3. Topstitch around the edges to secure the fabric. *Fig. B*

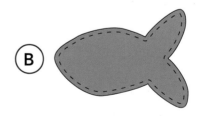

4. Hand stitch the small button eyes on the fish and the flamingo. See the pattern for placement.

5. Fold the inside pocket in half, right sides together, to make a 5½″ × 6½″ rectangle. Iron the woven interfacing to one side. Sew around outer edge, leaving a 3″ opening for turning. *Fig. C*

6. Iron the woven interfacing to the wrong side of both lining pieces.

7. Place the pocket 1½″ down from the top and centered on 1 lining piece. Sew around the 3 sides at ¼″ and again at ⅛″ from the pocket edges. *Fig. D*

8. Stitch the 2 strap pieces together to make a 53½″ length. Iron the interfacing to the center of this strap. Iron interfacing to the center of 2 tab pieces. *Fig. E*

9. Fold the short ends of the long strap in ¼″ and press. Fold both long sides of the long strap in to the edges of the interfacing and press. Fold the strap in half lengthwise and press. Topstitch around the outer edge to secure the edges of the strap. *Fig. F*

10. Fold the short ends of the tabs in ¼″ and press. Fold both long sides over the interfacing and fold in half lengthwise; press. Pin to hold. Topstitch around the outer edge.

11. Thread the long strap through the slide of the brass double loop and back out the other side. Place the end onto the strap and sew across several times to secure it. *Fig. G*

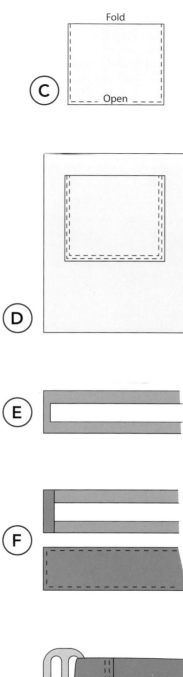

12. Slide 1 clip onto the strap and send the strap back through on the front of the slide. Add the remaining clip to the remaining strap end, fold over approximately ½˝, and sew. *Fig. H*

13. Slide the short tabs through the D-rings and fold them in half. Pin to secure and set aside. *Fig. I*

14. Fold in the short ends of the zipper tab pieces ¼˝. Then fold in half and press.

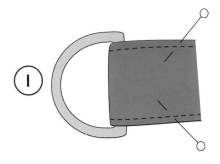

15. Place the tab onto the zipper at the end, just past the end of the teeth. Stitch across. Trim the zipper if necessary and add the remaining tab so that the zipper plus the tabs measures 9˝. *Fig. J*

16. Start with the bag front right side up on your work surface. Place the zipper, teeth down, across the top of the fabric with the zipper centered. Pin in place. *Fig. K*

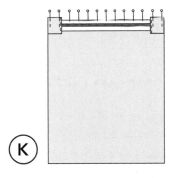

17. Place the piece of lining fabric without the pocket right side down on top of the pinned zipper. Make sure to match the top and side edges of the outer shell and lining. Pin the lining in place. *Fig. L*

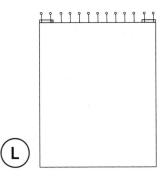

18. Sew using the zipper foot on your machine. *Fig. M*

19. Measure in ½˝ on each side at the top of the outer shell back fabric. Pin the small straps and D-rings at the marks, with the rings and straps facing inward.

20. Fold the fabric back from the zipper so that the outer shell and lining are wrong sides together. Place the remaining side of the zipper facedown on the right side of the remaining outer shell piece. Pin in place.

21. Place the lining right side down on top of the zipper. Make sure to match the top and side edges of the outer shell lining fabrics. Pin and sew in place.

22. Pin the piping around the 3 outer edges of the bag front, with the cord facing inward. Be sure to angle the piping off the top of each side. *Fig. N*

23. Arrange and pin the right sides of the outer fabric together and the lining pieces together. Sew around the outer edges, leaving an approximate 4˝ opening at the bottom of the lining for turning and hand stitching. *Fig. O*

24. Clip the corners and turn right side out. Press the edges flat. Hand stitch the lining opening closed. Push the lining into the purse through the zipper.

25. Clip the strap to the D-rings.

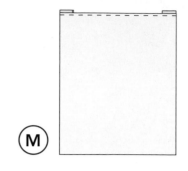

(M)

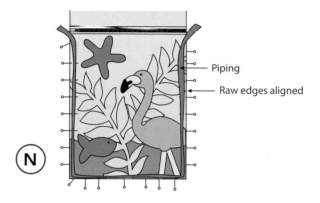

(N)

Piping

Raw edges aligned

(O)

Open

flip-flop travel bag ......

FINISHED SIZE: 9½" × 14"

materials

- ⅓ yard of light-colored quilting cotton for outer shell

- ⅓ yard of quilting cotton for lining

- ¼ yard of quilting cotton for pull cord and flip-flop appliqué

- ¼ yard of quilting cotton for casing and "Life" appliqué

- 2″ × 2″ quilting cotton for shell appliqué

- 3″ × 3″ quilting cotton for starfish appliqué

- 4″ × 4″ quilting cotton for flip-flop strap appliqué

- ⅛ yard of paper-backed fusible webbing

- ⅓ yard of pom-pom trim

- Disappearing ink pen

cutting

OUTER SHELL

- 2 pieces 10″ × 13″

LINING

- 2 pieces 10″ × 13″

PULL CORD

- 1 piece 4″ × 42″

CASING

- 2 pieces 4″ × 10½″

instructions

Seam allowances are ¼˝.

1. Transfer the embroidery design (pattern pullout page P1) onto the bag front piece.

2. Trace the Flip-Flop Travel Bag appliqué patterns (pullout page P1) onto the paper side of the fusible web.

3. Cut out the fusible web approximately ¼˝ outside the drawn line. Place the appliqué fabric right side down on the ironing board. Place the fusible web, paper side up, on top of the fabric. Be sure the fabric is larger the fusible web. To protect your iron, cover the fusible web with a nonstick pressing cloth. Follow the manufacturer's instructions to adhere the web to the fabric. Repeat for each piece of the appliqué pattern. Cut the pieces out on the pattern lines and remove the paper backing. Arrange all pieces on the bag front, keeping them at least ¼˝ inside the edge. Iron in place. *Fig. A*

4. Using black thread, topstitch around the edges of the appliqué to secure the fabric. Sew over the tracing of the words and scrolls. (Dropping the feed dogs on your machine and using a free-motion foot is helpful for this step, but not necessary.) If you miss an edge or get a little wobbly, stitch back over that part. There is nothing wrong with going over the stitches a few times; it adds detail.

5. Fold in one of the short casing ends ¼˝, and then fold again another ¼˝. Press and sew. Repeat this step for the second piece of casing fabric. *Fig. B*

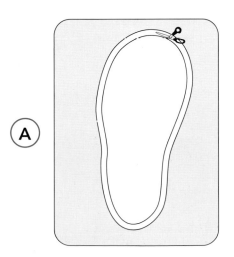

(A)

(B)

6. Place the casing facedown on the front outer shell; align the top edges. The turned end should be on the left. Sew across the top and press. Sew the second casing to the top edge of the back outer shell, making sure the folded edge is on the right. *Fig. C*

7. On both bag sides, sew the opposite side of the casing to the lining. Press the seams open. *Fig. D*

8. Open up and align the outer shell and the lining pieces. Pin the pom-pom trim along the bottom of the outer shell pieces, with the balls facing inward. Sew, starting at the bottom of the lining and skipping the turned edges. Leave a 4″ opening in the lining for turning. *Fig. E*

9. Turn right side out and hand stitch the opening in the lining closed. Push the lining into the bag. Press the top edge so that the casing is folded in half. Topstitch around the bottom of the casing. *Fig. F*

10. Fold the pull cord in half lengthwise, right sides facing. Using scissors, cut the corner off each end to make a curve. Sew all of the way around, leaving a 4″ opening along the side for turning. Turn right side out, press, and hand stitch the opening closed. *Fig. G*

11. Using a safety pin, thread the cord through the channel of the bag. Tie a bow to close the bag when it is in use.

(C)

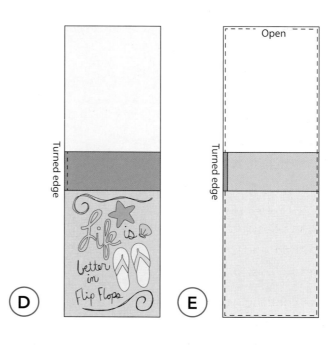

(D) (E)

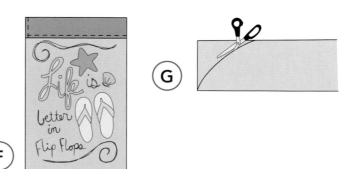

(F) (G)

about the author

It all started when Jennifer was four years old and received a Sew Perfect sewing machine. Her grandmother gave her a stack of upholstery fabric samples, and Jennifer jumped right into sewing. In high school her first job was at a fabric store, so she could basically spend her paycheck on more fabric. Her love of sewing has never stopped.

Jennifer received her BFA in ceramics from Indiana University in 1995. A year later she started her own business, selling ceramic tiles, beads, and jewelry. At age 36 she decided it was time for a change, and she moved on to designing fabric, making ceramic buttons, and designing sewing patterns.

Jennifer continues to design fabric as well as other licensed products, and she sells sewing patterns and kits under the name Jennifer Jangles. She celebrated her twentieth year of being a self-supporting artist in 2016. This is her second book with C&T Publishing.

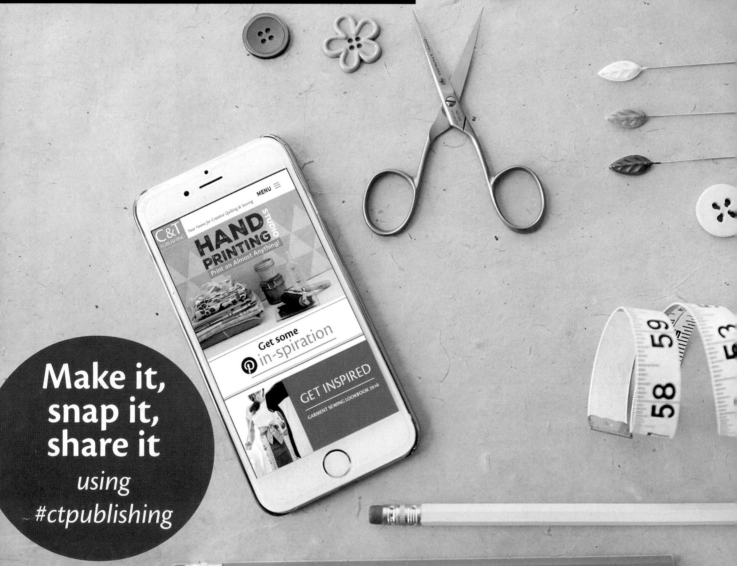

Want even more creative content?